English after the Fall

ROBERT SCHOLES

English after the Fall

From Literature to Textuality

UNIVERSITY OF IOWA PRESS | IOWA CITY

University of Iowa Press, Iowa City 52242
Copyright © 2011 by the University of Iowa Press
www.uiowapress.org
Printed in the United States of America
Design by Sara T. Sauers

The University of Iowa Press is a member of Green Press Initiative
and is committed to preserving natural resources.
Printed on acid-free paper

Library of Congress Cataloging-in-Publication Data
Scholes, Robert, 1929–
English after the fall : from literature to textuality / Robert Scholes.
    p.   cm.
Includes bibliographical references and index.
ISBN-13: 978-1-60938-055-7 (pbk.)
ISBN-10: 1-60938-055-x (pbk.)
1. English philology—Study and teaching.   I. Title.
PE65.S36 2011
807.1′1—dc22   2011013863

THIS BOOK IS DEDICATED TO CARL H. KLAUS, my first friend in graduate school, later my valued colleague at the University of Iowa, and my collaborator in various textbooks. We have been teaching one another and learning from one another for more than fifty years. And the last thing I learned from Carl is that the University of Iowa Press would be the right place for this book. Thank you, for everything, Carl.

Teaching is sharing, a function of generosity.
—*Hugh Kenner*

CONTENTS

ACKNOWLEDGMENTS

IN A LIFETIME OF LEARNING AND TEACHING THE DEBTS PILE up—to authors, teachers, students—too many to be acknowledged. One can only hope that one's own work in these roles has reduced the balance a bit. However, for this particular book a number of people have made direct contributions that must be recognized, saving me from blunders, encouraging me to address certain issues, and helping me give this book its proper shape. I received this kind of help from Gerald Graff, Carl Klaus, Sean Latham, Rosmarie Waldrop, Lori Lefkovitz, Shannon McLachlan, Jo Ann Scholes, Stephen Barney, Jonathan Goldman, David Barney, Joseph Parsons, and Jeanette Nakada. I am very grateful to all of them. I will acknowledge some sources of special importance at the end of this book.

English after the Fall

> Som natural tears they drop'd, but wip'd them soon;
> The World was all before them, where to choose
> Thir place of rest, and Providence thir guide:
> They hand in hand with wandring steps and slow,
> Through *Eden* took thir solitarie way.
> —The last lines of *Paradise Lost*, 1667 edition

WITH THOSE MEMORABLE WORDS JOHN MILTON CONCLUDED his epic justification of the human condition—a blind old man, dictating to dutiful daughters. I am no Milton, just a slightly deaf old man, typing on a computer keyboard, but I, too, have written about a fall: the fall of English as a field of study. The Fall Milton described came about because Adam and Eve became obsessed with and finally consumed a forbidden fruit. The fall of English came about because of the alluring but ultimately fatal choice of literature as the central object of the English curriculum. In a previous book, *The Rise and Fall of English*, I attempted to describe this situation. I am trying again in this sequel for a number of reasons.

When Milton wrote a sequel to *Paradise Lost*, he called it *Paradise Regained*, but my sequel cannot bear such a title. This field cannot regain what it has lost. No savior can reopen the gates to paradise for English studies, which will have to survive in the real world. This book is simply a profession of faith in that fallen field of studies and an attempt to suggest a direction for its future. This effort began, however, not with Milton's epic but with a situation described in a more humble text published half a century before *Paradise Lost*. In part 2 of *Don Quixote*, the Don and Sancho Panza find themselves in a world where part 1 is already circulating, making things complicated for them in interesting ways. I wrote about this years ago, but now I know from direct experience something of how they must have felt, for I have lived for some years in a world where my earlier description of the rise and fall of English was being taught and studied, especially in classes for future English teachers. A number of such students have contacted me with embarrassing questions, such as whether I knew of any departments that were following my advice for making the fall of English a fortunate one.

The honest answer to that question is that I do not know of any such departments. This is, no doubt, because I failed to make the case persuasively enough, but there is also another reason. Thomas Kuhn taught us long ago that a shift in the paradigms that drive a discipline does not come about through persuasion of those with settled views, but through their replacement by younger people with more open minds. In the case of English departments, graduate students are still being prepared in the old way—as specialists in narrow domains of literature—but the world they encounter when they leave graduate school is often shockingly different from the one they have been prepared to inhabit. Even those lucky enough to prepare in a special field and find a job teaching a course in their specialty are discovering that the shape of the larger field is changing. And many young people with PhD's in English never find jobs in their special fields, ending up in part-time or temporary positions, if not out of the profession altogether. The larger field is changing shape, and these young men and women know it. Much of what English departments do now is largely perceived as peripheral to college and university education if not utterly useless. Enrollments in advanced courses in literature are falling, and the number of English majors is declining in most schools. The fall of English is actually part of the fall of all the humanities in a world that is driven by technological progress and the bottom line. In such a world the humanities must demonstrate their usefulness in order to survive as more than tokens of gentility. As the most universally used language in this world, English has enormous potential as a field of study, but, to exploit this potential, English faculties will have to face some difficult realities and make some major changes.

The academic fields that are flourishing today are those that offer training in marketable skills, like computer science, chemistry, biology, and engineering. The humanities, in general, are having trouble competing in this world—not because they are useless but because they have been reluctant to define themselves in terms of use. In the case of English, the more obviously useful features of the field have been relegated to the bottom of the reward system, where courses in rhetoric and composition are taught, for the most part, by graduate students and part-time faculty. Simply reversing this structure is an impossible dream, though some rhetoricians do indeed imagine it happening. What is needed, as I understand the situation, is a broader reconsideration of the purpose of English studies. We need to see the main function of English departments as helping students become better users of the language—basically, better readers and writers. Literary works have a role to play in this function, but they are a means to, not the end of, studies in English, though they have often been treated as the end. In this book, I want to make the case for a shift in the field—from privileging literature to studying a wide range of texts in a wide range of media—so that what I call "textuality" can become the main concern of English departments.

The rest of this book will be devoted to explaining and attempting to justify that position, starting with this brief reminder of how we got where we are. The study of English as an academic field and the rise of departments devoted to that study happened in colleges and universities just a century or so ago, with English departments replacing departments of rhetoric and drawing students away from classical studies. This history has been discussed by Gerald Graff and others, including myself, and I will not repeat it here, except to emphasize that the rise of English departments coincided with a particular cultural phenomenon—the emergence of modernism in literature and the other arts. The new field of English needed something to compete with the rigor of classical and philological studies, and modernism provided just what was needed. Because modernist works like *Ulysses* and *The Waste Land* needed explaining, this whole new discipline of English became oriented to explication, with texts difficult enough to require academic interpretation becoming privileged in our classrooms, including complex older works, like the metaphysical poems of John Donne. Critics like T. S. Eliot, F. R. Leavis, and I. A. Richards led the way, and American academics followed them, as did British and Canadian professors in this new field. We can see modernism and its effects more clearly now, because it is over, and its end is contributing to the decline of literary studies in general.

When English literature replaced rhetoric as the center of the field, the study of textual power was put in a subordinate role from which it has never emerged. And when explication of difficult literary texts became the main form in which reading was taught, the enjoyment of textual pleasure was also subordinated. But this was a time when major literary and artistic figures were celebrities on a grand scale—writers from Oscar Wilde to Gertrude Stein and F. T. Marinetti were newsworthy, and debates about imagism, futurism, cubism, and vorticism extended beyond the little magazines to the popular press. The importance of literature inspired the editors and writers who worked for such modernist little magazines as the *Egoist* and the *Little Review*, and for larger journals like *Scribner's* and the *Atlantic Monthly* as well. But literary works are no longer so central in our culture. Film, television, and digital celebrities dominate the culture, now, with literature and its makers in a less visible position, though a writer can have a few minutes of fame if Oprah notices her or him. Good literary work is still being produced, of course, but the modernist privileging of difficulty as a sign of value has faded. And excellent work in other media clamors for attention. The cultural dominance of the newer media is not simply a matter of celebrity. It is a matter of what people attend to in their moments of leisure—what they read, look at, or listen to, and what they remember and talk about with their friends and co-workers. This is a complicated situation, which I shall consider more fully in later chapters, but first I must explain how my own experience has shaped my views.

I have been an English teacher for more than fifty years, but English is not the only departmental structure I have inhabited. For the past thirty years I have also been in a Department of Comparative Literature, and, twenty years ago I helped to found, and shepherd through administrative barriers, a Department of Modern Culture and Media, which is my present base of operations. I never meant to be a "comparatist," but I studied Latin from the seventh grade through the twelfth, had a couple of years of French in high school, a bit of Spanish in college, worked on my French while in the Navy, took some German in graduate school to pass an exam, picked up some Italian through my interest in opera, and acquired the rudiments of ancient Greek while doing postdoctoral work in Wisconsin. None of this made me what I think of as a "real" comparatist, since I was scarcely fluent in any of those tongues. What led me toward comparative literature was my interest in narratives of all sorts, and my specialization in modern British and American literature. Anyone who works on writers like Joyce, Eliot, and Pound discovers that they were comparatists, who produced work that requires those who study them to move in that direction. And anyone interested in narrative discovers that there are important narrative texts in languages around the world.

As a modernist scholar with an interest in narrative, I felt that the study of film was crucial for any university or college. And, since Brown had no particular place for that study when I got there in 1970, I helped to start a program that ultimately became a department in which film, and later television and digital media, could be studied in a disciplined way, though I never thought of myself as an expert in the more contemporary media. In this new department I taught courses in semiotic theory, literary and artistic modernism, textuality, and opera, leaving the teaching of film and television to colleagues more expert in those fields. And I continued to teach writing at all levels. I mention all these tedious personal details because I want to claim that they have given me a special perspective for the proposals I want to make about the proper direction for English studies after the fall.

At the end of *Paradise Lost*, Milton said of his fallen humans that "the World was all before them, where to choose"—and we should take heart from that. We have it in our power to choose—not a "place of rest," but a direction for English that suits the fallen world we live in. The rest of this book will be an argument for choosing what I call "textuality" as the focus of study and teaching appropriate for English departments—which means replacing literature as the main object of attention. It is not that English teachers need to reject the value of literariness or ignore the great works that they love and honor. But they need to expand their horizons, to look more widely for literariness, and study textual power and pleasure wherever they exist. In what follows, I will begin by looking at the history of the word *literature* itself, and then move on to a demonstration of how a constricted notion of literature contributes to the fragmentation of the field, limiting what can be taught and how this teaching is done. This will lead to a discussion of the expanded field of textuality, followed by illustrative considerations of two sorts of texts that are presently considered to be largely outside the field of English, for quite different reasons: those that

I call sacred and profane. If such texts can be brought into English classrooms successfully, English teachers may yet find satisfaction working in this fallen world.

English after the Fall

CHAPTER ONE

Literature and Its Others

Literature IS A WORD THAT HAS HAD DIFFERENT MEANINGS AT different times in the English language, and no one should be more aware of this history than those of us who study and teach that language. But all too often we behave as if the present meaning of the word had been permanently assigned to it by Adam in the Garden of Eden when he was naming the beasts as God instructed him to do. In this chapter I would like to untangle the story of that word, as clearly as I can, so that English teachers may more easily free themselves from its domination. The word *literature* entered our language in the fourteenth century, coming from the Latin *litteratura*, which, in that language, referred directly to letters, as in the Greek alphabet, or to texts made of letters, or, indirectly, to learning based on such texts (see Lewis and Short). When it became a word in Middle English, it replaced the Old English term *boccræft* (book skill). There is no definition of literature in Dr. Johnson's *Dictionary*, though he uses the word often in that work and elsewhere.

One of the meanings of the word in Johnson's time was simply a text that could move an audience or earn money from a publisher, as when Johnson praised the play of his friend Goldsmith—*She Stoops to Conquer*: "I know of no comedy for many years that has so much exhilarated an audience, that has answered so much the great end of comedy—making an audience merry." Goldsmith himself made a very revealing comment about what a literary reputation meant in a conversation recorded by Boswell: "I consider an author's literary reputation to be alive only while his name will ensure a good price for his copy from the booksellers. I will get you (to Johnson) a hundred guineas for any thing whatever that you shall write, if you put your name to it." Both these observations were made in 1773 at a gathering of what was known as "The Literary Club," and they suggest a notion of literature that was not very exalted, pointing toward the pleasure of audiences and the commercial value of an author's name as literary qualities. But this notion was to change over the next two centuries. To understand this shifting sense of what the word *literature* might refer to, we need to look both backward and forward from that point in the later eighteenth century.

This is a complex matter, and I must ask for some indulgence as I try to work through it, starting with a look back toward earlier notions of literature and what was literary. In the seventeenth century, when these matters were first addressed in magazines, literature meant serious discussions of various topics—and poetry was not considered serious. William Graham described this situation in his book *The Beginnings of English Literary Periodicals*, directing our attention to "the seventeenth-century feeling that poetry was always somehow associated with flippancy and vice." He also reminded us that other sorts of texts we now consider literary were actually disdained by serious thinkers in the seventeenth century, with one editor observing that, in his periodicals, he could not mention "plays, satyrs, Romances and the like," since they were "fitter to corrupt men's morals, and to shake the grounds of natural religion, than to promote learning and piety." The very genres that we now think of as exclusively literary—drama, fiction, and poetry—were once excluded from serious literature in the minds of scholars and critics. The clearly serious epic poetry of Milton, and the growing appreciation of Shakespeare, had much to do with changing these attitudes in England, as did the discussions of these texts in magazines like the *Spectator*.

When we think of the great intellectual developments leading to the modern era, we are usually aware of the rise of science and the gradual emergence of the scientific fields that we now recognize, like biology and chemistry, during the eighteenth and nineteenth centuries. We are often less aware, I believe, that our modern notion of art evolved during the same period. Both of these developments have their roots in the Renaissance, but did not become fully codified until the Enlightenment. There were scientists like Galileo in the Renaissance, and Vasari's *Lives of the Most Excellent Painters, Sculptors, and Architects* (Le Vite delle più eccellenti pittori, scultori, ed architettori) was first published in 1550. But the codification of the sciences did not really get under way in Europe until the British Royal Society was established in 1660, and the first English translation of Vasari's *Lives* did not appear until twenty-five years later in 1685. In fact, the formal study of art in the new philosophical field called "aesthetics" was not named until Baumgarten took it up in the 1730s, and the word *aesthetics* itself did not enter the English language until a century later. By then Kant, Schiller, and Hegel had written on the beautiful and the arts, and in Britain Edmund Burke had produced an influential work, *A Philosophical Enquiry into the Origin of Our Ideas of the Sublime and Beautiful*, in 1757. Burke's book and David Hume's essay "On the Standard of Taste," published in that same year, changed everything.

This change took two forms that are crucial to the history of the concept of literature. One of these forms can be located in the three volumes of lectures by Lord Kames, published in 1762 and titled *Elements of Criticism*. Following Hume, Kames took up the question of taste in his introduction and returned to it in the final lecture. Arguing in the introduction that "the God of nature" has constructed the world so that humans may pass from "corporeal pleasures to the more refined pleasures of sense; and not less so, from these to the exalted pleasures of morality and religion," he continued in this vein:

We stand therefore engaged in honour, as well as interest, to second the purposes of nature, by cultivating the pleasures of the eye and ear, those especially that require extraordinary culture, such as are inspired by poetry, painting, sculpture, music, gardening, and architecture. *This chiefly is the duty of the opulent, who have leisure to improve their minds and their feelings.* . . . a taste in the fine arts goes hand in hand with the moral sense, to which indeed it is nearly allied. Both of them discover what is right and wrong. . . . they are rooted in human nature. (emphasis added)

It is painfully clear how powerfully the social and economic are commingled with the aesthetic and moral in this formulation. Human nature reaches its peak among the opulent, who have the leisure to cultivate their taste. And good taste is closely connected to good behavior, making the rich not just richer but better human beings than their inferiors in opulence. The binary opposition of leisure and work, between gentleman and tradesman, ran deep in British culture and is scarcely eradicated even now.

The question of taste is connected to a popular term used at this period to designate certain texts of a particular sort: *belles lettres*. Borrowed from the French, this expression had entered the English language by the middle of the eighteenth century. In his *Dictionary* of 1755, Johnson defined it as "polite literature," which was thus distinguished from writing that was more practical or scientific—writing which did not involve the question of good taste. The word *belles* can be translated as Johnson did—as "polite"—or, more literally, as "beautiful." Belles lettres was used in the second half of the eighteenth century, then, to refer to certain texts we would now call literary, but in a sense that was tied to leisure and politeness in a way that more recent definitions of literature would disdain. And this is where that other crucial work of 1757 comes in. In his *Philosophical Enquiry into the Origin of Our Ideas of the Sublime and Beautiful*, Edmund Burke had distinguished between two kinds of aesthetic function: the sublime and the beautiful. This distinction, which was taken up and refined by Immanuel Kant, effectively undermined the notion of belles lettres, because Burke defined two orders of verbal art—a higher and a lower—with mere beauty (or politeness) assigned to the lower level. And this led the way to the next development in the history of our concept of literature.

Burke's "beautiful," and the "beautiful" of those who followed him, had to do with order, regularity, and ease—something like politeness. His "sublime" had to do with more extreme emotions, such as fear and awe. A version of this distinction operates powerfully in English Romantic poetry, as a difference between "fancy" and "imagination," with "fancy" playing a lower role than imagination in the definitions of Wordsworth and Coleridge, with Coleridge explicitly linking the imagination of poets (in his *Biographia Literaria*) to the divine power that created the world itself, while relegating poetic fancy to a pleasant but earthbound faculty:

> The Imagination then I consider either as primary, or secondary. The primary Imagination I hold to be the living power and prime agent of all human perception, and as a repetition in the finite mind of the eternal act of creation in the infinite I AM. The secondary Imagination I consider as an echo of the former, co-existing with the conscious will, yet still as identical with the primary in the kind of its agency, and differing only in degree, and in the mode of its operation. It dissolves, diffuses, dissipates, in order to recreate: or where this process is rendered impossible, yet still at all events it struggles to idealize and to unify. It is essentially vital, even as all objects (as objects) are essentially fixed and dead.
>
> FANCY, on the contrary, has no other counters to play with, but fixities and definites. The fancy is indeed no other than a mode of memory emancipated from the order of time and space; while it is blended with, and modified by that empirical

phaenomenon of the will, which we express by the word Choice. But equally with the ordinary memory the Fancy must receive all its materials ready made from the law of association.

Literature was then redefined as referring to works of the Coleridgean Imagination, which meant mainly serious poetical works and works of tragic drama that approached the sublime and captured painful aspects of human experience—what Matthew Arnold would call "high seriousness." Through this process, in the first half of the nineteenth century, literature moved much closer to the concept understood by most English teachers today as governing their field of study. But it did not move all the way to our present concept of literature until a century later, because in Coleridge's time it was centered on poetry or poetical drama and tended to exclude fiction.

As a young man, I spent many hours in the secondhand bookstores of Fourth Avenue in Manhattan. They all had a "Literature" section and a "Fiction" section, a distinction one still finds in that vanishing tribe of shops. It was not until the end of the nineteenth century that a persuasive case was made for the inclusion of fiction (or some fiction) in the literary category. The issue came up when John Morley established the "English Men of Letters" series of books in 1878, which grudgingly included a few writers of fiction as "men of letters." As F. J. M. Korsten put it, in an article on this series, "For the higher critics the novel was intellectually not satisfying, and their attitude to the novel was often very condescending." In his book *On the Study of Literature* Morley himself expressed his regret about the popularity of the novel and he argued that it would be better if the novel received less and "general literature" more attention. In the volume on Samuel Richardson in that series, Austin Dobson called that novelist a "Complete English Tradesman" and complained that "most of his characters are in the habit of morbidly interrogating their internal mechanism." Samuel

Johnson, as it happens, had favorably compared Richardson to his contemporary and rival, Henry Fielding, by observing "that there was as great a difference between them as between a man who knew how a watch was made and one who could tell the hour by looking on the dial-plate," and Dobson seemed to be recalling that watch, though ignoring Johnson's view that to understand human character—as opposed to manners—"a man must dive into the recesses of the human heart."

It is ironic that Dobson objected to the very thing that was about to make the modern novel unmistakably "literary"—the inward turn toward subjectivity that we find in the works of James, Conrad, Ford, Joyce, Woolf, and the other important modern novelists. Until then, fiction had been outside the realm of literature in the minds of critics and on the shelves of bookstores as well. We can date the inclusion of fiction among the arts with some precision to the last decades of the nineteenth century, triggered by two pamphlets called *The Art of Fiction*. The first, by Walter Besant, was a lecture delivered and published in 1884, and the second was a response by Henry James, written in that same year. Besant's major argument was introduced at the beginning of his lecture, where he argued that "Fiction is an Art in every way worthy to be called the sister and the equal of the Arts of Painting, Sculpture, Music, and Poetry; that is to say, her field is as boundless, her possibilities as vast, her excellences as worthy of admiration, as may be claimed for any of her sister Arts."

Henry James's response to Besant is usually regarded as the demolition of an amateurish essay by a powerful professional, and so it is to some extent, but there are also points of agreement between the two writers. James agreed, for instance, on the necessity for making the claim that fiction should be taken seriously. Here is how he put it, speaking of Besant's assertion that fiction should be considered an art:

It is excellent that he should have struck this note, for his doing so indicates that there was a need of it, that his proposition may be to many people a novelty. One rubs one's eyes at the thought; but the rest of Mr. Besant's essay confirms the revelation. I suspect in truth that it would be possible to confirm it still further, and that one would not be far wrong in saying that in addition to the people to whom it has never occurred that a novel ought to be artistic, there are many others who, if this principle were urged upon them, would be filled with indefinable mistrust.

James, writing at the moment when the aesthetic movement was reaching its apogee, felt that discussing fiction as an art would disturb some people. But he took the lead in doing just this, which is one reason why an ultramodernist magazine, the *Little Review*, devoted an entire issue to him in 1918, with articles by Ezra Pound and T. S. Eliot, among others. James's own remarks on other novelists like Balzac are full of comments on the need for imagination to transform reporting and recording into something more artistic—remarks that foreshadow Virginia Woolf's criticism of Arnold Bennett in "Mr. Bennett and Mrs. Brown" some decades later.

We may say, then, that fiction ceased to be one of literature's others or opposites in the later nineteenth century, being replaced by a new other that actually tainted some works of fiction, though not all. This new other was journalism, especially what came to be called the "new journalism" in the 1880s. This is not to be confused with the American "new journalism" of the 1960s, though it is similar enough in certain respects to be considered an earlier version of the same phenomenon: an enlivening personalization of journalistic prose. This is the way T. P. O'Connor described it in the *New Review* in 1889:

Beyond doubt we are on the eve of a new departure in English journalism. All the new journals adopt the new methods, and even the oldest and the most staid, cautiously and tentatively, and with a certain air of self-reproach, admit some of the features of the New Journalism. Before the revolution is finally accomplished, it is well, perhaps, to argue the questions which lie at the root of the difference between the old style and the new.

O'Connor went on to do just what he promised, pointing out the virtues of "the more personal tone" of the new journalism, including reporting on the tone and background of political speeches, rather than just printing the words. And he went on to make this prophetic statement: "No one's life is now private; the private dinner party, the intimate conversation, all are told. If this kind of thing go on, say the critics of modern journalism, we shall before long be in the same plight as the journalism of America." O'Connor worried about going too far in this direction, but he could not stop the process that has led us to where we are now, and he did not foresee the new media that would bring the transgressions of celebrities and politicians into our homes every minute of the day.

The "New Journalism" of the 1880s was in fact just a continuation of a process that had been going on for some time and has continued steadily, being renamed with the same name at intervals. This process caught fiction in its web and left it contaminated. The connection to journalism and to the circulating libraries was noted by Coleridge in his lectures on Shakespeare and Milton around 1812:

I will run the risk of asserting, that where the reading of novels prevails as a habit, it occasions in time the entire destruction of the powers of the mind; it is such an utter loss to the reader, that it is not so much to be called pass-time as kill-time. It conveys no trustworthy information as to facts; it produces no improvement of the intellect, but fills the mind with a mawkish and morbid sensibility, which is directly hostile to the cultivation, invigoration and enlargement of the nobler faculties of the understanding.

In the work of Q. D. and F. R. Leavis, especially around 1930, we find them following Coleridge, which led to the Leavises putting journalism and popular fiction in a lower category, outside the exclusive literary realm. From this perspective, literature improves the mind, while journalism and popular fiction degrade it. The modern world had produced what F. R. Leavis called, in a pamphlet of that name, *Mass Civilization and Minority Culture*—and Culture, in this view, trumps Civilization. In this pamphlet, Leavis aligned himself with Ezra Pound, quoting approvingly from Pound's *How to Read*: "Save in the rare and limited instances of invention in the plastic arts, or in mathematics, the individual cannot think and communicate his thought, the governor and legislator cannot act effectively or frame his laws, without words, and the solidity and validity of those words is in the care of the damned and despised *literati*." Pound and the Leavises agreed about the degrading effects of popular journalism, and the importance of promoting uses of language at the opposite end of a spectrum of value—the literary end. But their definitions were not generically based. That is, they did not define literature as all writing in poetic forms or any other kind of form. For them, all good writing, including essays and the novels of Lawrence (for Leavis) and Joyce (for Pound) counted as literature, though popular fiction did not.

The academic departments of English and other modern languages that arose at the end of the nineteenth century needed to define their territory and establish their seriousness, so as to challenge the rigor of studying the Latin and Greek classics. They solved this problem for a time by emphasizing philology, which evolved into linguistics, and, in a more durable way, by concentrating on the study of a canon composed of serious poetry, drama, and fiction. The critic/teachers in these new departments of English borrowed from the modernist writers the notion of literature as a form of art. James Joyce's autobiographical novel was called *A Portrait of the Artist as a Young Man* because Stephen Dedalus is going to be a literary artist like Joyce himself. The pages of the small magazines of modernism, like the *Egoist*, *Poetry*, and the *Little Review* are studded with definitions of literature as an art. And the intellectual history of modernism can be traced in the movement from these magazines to the more purely critical *Criterion* of T. S. Eliot and the ultracritical *Scrutiny* of the Leavises, who took the teaching of English seriously. This process enshrined the New Criticism in English departments in the United States as the study of verbal art, leading the faculties of those departments further and further away from the concerns of rhetoric and textuality, and further away from texts that did not proclaim their artistic status and demonstrate it by the difficulties they posed for readers. What Johnson had called "making an audience merry" was not one of their concerns—and we are still suffering from that.

Among other things, this attitude led to a complete break between departments of English and Journalism, in the print media, and between English and the audiovisual media, as well. It also raised a barrier between the teaching of literature and the teaching of writing. These divisions in the field are making it difficult for us to solve our problems because they prevent English departments from offering the kind of unified studies that their students want and need. The idea that popular fiction could not also be good literature led F. R. Leavis to exclude Dickens from his "great tradition" of English novelists. It also led Ezra Pound, when he joined the editorial staff of the *Little Review*, to persuade the editors to add on the cover of every issue this statement: "MAKING NO COMPROMISE WITH THE PUBLIC TASTE." This notion that popular works cannot be worthy of serious study is one of the literary myths we need to reject. Many works in the new media, and other texts excluded from the realm of literature, when it is narrowly defined, are serious and powerful. They are also interesting. And among them are texts that use language in ways that cry out to be recognized as literary—if, by literary we mean language used vigorously or subtly to stimulate thought and feeling.

What the critics of mass civilization feared was language used to provoke feeling without thought, and they saw this as characteristic of popular forms like "railway novels," illustrated magazines, and motion pictures. Q. D. Leavis looked back to a golden Elizabethan Age when "the masses were receiving their amusement from above (instead of being specially catered for by journalists, film-directors, and popular novelists, as they are now)." She was forgetting, perhaps, that Shakespeare was just an actor who wrote scripts for his fellow players, very much like the makers of films that she condemned. While it is certainly true that feeling without thought can be dangerous, the wholesale condemnation of genres and media is a blunt instrument used where something more precise is needed. Such condemnations are guilty of the sin they are excoriating. They are not thoughtful enough to recognize the range of quality that we may find in any genre or medium. We need to stretch the notion of literariness to include signs that are not verbal. Everything in a text that carries meaning is a sign, including visual representations of events and music that influences our perceptions of what we see. The moment in the film *Casablanca* when the French police officer says that he is "shocked, shocked" to find that gambling is going on at Rick's café, while visibly pocketing his winnings from the roulette table, provides us with a text at once verbal and visual that is as memorable as any moment in Shakespeare. It is thoroughly literary without being literature.

Have we settled the meaning of that elusive word, *literature*? I hope not. I hope we have unsettled it. Thanks to Jonathan Rose's extremely useful book, *The Intellectual Life of the British Working Classes*, we know how a range of texts from Shakespeare, Bunyan and Scott to Carlyle, Ruskin, and Macaulay helped to stimulate the minds of weavers and miners who rose to higher social and political positions in the nineteenth century. That is, writers of plays and parables, along with a range of other genres, all contributed to the feeling for language that opened the world of intellectual exchange to people who had been shut off from it. Again and again, readers of that time have recorded how the power and the music of words changed their lives, whether their reading was "imaginative" literature or essayistic, whether it was fiction, history, or criticism. All the texts that move us or instruct us should be included in our field, rather than a set of texts limited by some narrowly defined notion of literature. Our most powerful media mix verbal language with visual signs and even musical themes: Richard Wagner's "total work of art" (*Gesamtkunstwerk*), with a vengeance. We live in a world dominated by mixed media rather than by different spheres partitioned off from one another. The purely verbal is not enough to explain it. Verbal signs have always had their music. What else is poetry all about? And words have always painted pictures, from the *eos rhododaktylos* (rosy-fingered dawn) of Homer to the "petals on a wet, black bough" of Pound. Pictures, and musical sounds as well, also evoke words though they cannot utter them. But we currently live in an academic world constrained by a notion of literature that excludes interesting and important texts of all kinds.

CHAPTER TWO

The Limiting Concept of Literature

THE LIMITS OF OUR PREVAILING CONCEPT OF LITERATURE first came to my attention in the course of editing, with some colleagues, a set of readings for college students of writing. This book was originally called *Fields of Writing*, but the publisher changed it to *Fields of Reading* at some point (inadvertently acknowledging, perhaps, the greater prestige of reading in English departments). We have been editing this book for years. It has readings in four rhetorical categories—Reflecting, Reporting, Explaining, and Arguing—and it ranges over all the academic fields, from science to art. Hence the title. For one edition, however, we added some works in those rhetorical categories that happened to be in verse—verse in the modes of reflecting, reporting, explaining, and arguing, to be sure, but clearly, unmistakably, verse—or poetry. Later we got back a survey on the use of the book in schools that adopted it. Some of the teachers surveyed welcomed the poetry, but others resisted it mightily. One, in particular, said that this introduction of what he called "literature" jeopardized the whole course, because the teachers would be teaching literature instead of composition. This opposition between the teaching of writing and the teaching of reading is one of the problems we need to solve, but we will not solve it until we can get beyond the notion of literature that motivated that reaction to the inclusion of poetry in this anthology.

In *Fields of Reading* we included poems because we found them reflecting, reporting, explaining, and arguing as well as any works in prose could do these things. For example, one poem we considered for inclusion in a subsequent edition of the book was this well-known work by Robert Frost:

Design
I found a dimpled spider, fat and white,
On a white heal-all, holding up a moth
Like a white piece of rigid satin cloth—
Assorted characters of death and blight
Mixed ready to begin the morning right,
Like the ingredients of a witches' broth—
A snow-drop spider, a flower like a froth,
And dead wings carried like a paper kite.

What had that flower to do with being white,
The wayside blue and innocent heal-all?
What brought the kindred spider to that height,
Then steered the white moth thither in the night?
What but design of darkness to appall?—
If design govern in a thing so small.

This poem by Robert Frost is a sonnet. That is, it was written in the most classic and literary form in the modern languages, going back to the moment these languages were first used for literary expression. There is no doubt, however, that it is also rhetoric. It is not some pure form of language designed to lead people away from reality toward aesthetic bliss, though it offers plenty of joy for those who like to see language handled with such mastery and precision. But this is an argument in a debate that has recently heated up in our culture—a debate about what is now called "Intelligent Design." In form, it is close to the one Francesco Petrarca used in the first decades of the fourteenth century, but Frost's form is even stricter, using only three rhyming sounds where Petrarch (as he is known in English) normally used four.

For rhetorical purposes, however, the octet of this sonnet is in the mode of reporting and the sestet in that of reflecting. That is, the first eight lines are a unit in which the speaker reports on what he found, and the last six lines are a unit in which he reflects on the meaning of that finding. And, as is so often the case with these rhetorical modes, this final reflection turns in the direction of argument. Three modes of rhetorical discourse in just fourteen lines. How could a teacher of rhetoric and composition ask for more? Frost's choice of words is dazzling, from the "dimpled" spider and the flower like a "froth" in the octet to that tension between "darkness" and "appall" in the closing couplet. "Appall," after all, means make pale, literally, and leave shaken, metaphorically. So we have "darkness" using whiteness to shock and awe the spectator of this "small" drama of life and death. We can also note that the simple word "white" is repeated in each of the first three lines—once for the spider, once for the flower, and once for the moth—and it is used again in the seventh line to point out that this flower is normally blue but not in this case. And it is this "unnatural" coloration—a minor miracle—that has triggered the event reported on in the octet, luring the moth to the spider's clutch.

This, in turn, leads Frost to address the question of whether the universe is the result of "design," and, ultimately, to the two linked questions that conclude the poem:

1. What power designed this appalling spectacle?
2. How far into the small things of this world can design extend?

The questions are in some sense rhetorical, but the poet does also offer an answer of sorts, though it is also a kind of further question. I hear an echo of William Blake's "The Tyger" in these lines, specifically of "What immortal hand or eye / Did frame thy fearful symmetry?" So, I read Frost's last lines this way:

If we reason back from these events to their presumed Designer, we find there not light but darkness, a darkness that disguises itself in white, the color of light, and uses a flower called a heal-all to lure a creature to its death. So the argument from design leads us to a Designer who is not a benevolent God but some sort of mischievous or malevolent figure—a Mephistopheles, perhaps.

I would not wish to insist that these lines be read this way. I think they are a bit too open for this kind of closure, perhaps, but I believe that they take us deep into the issues around the question of Intelligent Design, which are not merely "literary" issues but matters of philosophy or theology. Early drafts of the poem are available online, and they can lead us further into Frost's composing process. But what we need to notice here is that this poetry is performing intellectual work of a high order. Yet the notion of literature under which many members of our profession are operating works to prevent Frost's poem from being seen as the thoughtful, provocative thing it is. Which leads their students, I should think, to see poetry in the same way—as something that has no connection to their lives. Just think what it might do to the audience for poetry if students left English classes knowing that they might find food for thought and human feeling in the poems they encounter in magazines or on the Web rather than some literary emotion for which they have neither the time nor any need.

Poems are diminished if we confine them to our current restricted notion of literature. They are texts that are often meant to address real problems in the world, as Wordsworth clearly intended to do in writing about John Milton in his poem called "London, 1802":

> Milton! thou shouldst be living at this hour:
> England hath need of thee: she is a fen
> Of stagnant waters: altar, sword, and pen,

Fireside, the heroic wealth of hall and bower,
Have forfeited their ancient English dower
Of inward happiness. We are selfish men;
Oh! raise us up, return to us again;
And give us manners, virtue, freedom, power.

Thy soul was like a Star, and dwelt apart;
Thou hadst a voice whose sound was like the sea:
Pure as the naked heavens, majestic, free,
So didst thou travel on life's common way,
In cheerful godliness; and yet thy heart
The lowliest duties on herself did lay.

Wordsworth was addressing, in this poem, someone who had been dead for over a century, but speaking to him directly, as if he were a friend. This is a rhetorical move, since the poet clearly has another audience in mind—those he calls "we" and "us" in the poem. There is even a technical term for this kind of thing. It's called *apostrophe*—though it should not be confused with the punctuation mark that shares the name. Wordsworth pretends that he is talking to Milton, but he is not really talking to a dead poet. Still, "London, 1802" does indeed come to us indirectly, which means that we must read it two ways—and this, I would insist, is a skill that all readers need to master. Many utterances we encounter in the media are aimed at more than one audience, and we need to decode these as well as we can. But learning the subtleties of reading is just one of the rhetorical benefits of studying poetry. We can also learn from a poet like Wordsworth a lot about how persuasive discourse works—if we are willing to take his poem as the rhetorical creature it so clearly is.

Wordsworth, taken most directly, is asking Milton to return from the dead because his voice is needed. I'm sure Wordsworth believed in the afterlife, but I doubt if he expected Milton to answer his call—which might have put Wordsworth himself out of business, if he had. This dead end, so to speak, in the direct address of the poem, should send us with heightened interest to the indirect addressees, who are clearly his fellow citizens—of England and especially London—in the year 1802. And what is he telling them? His message is not cheerful. He says that virtually every aspect of life, from the most public (altar, sword, and pen) to the most private (Fireside, . . . hall and bower) has become tainted with unhappiness that is caused by selfishness, so that "manners, virtue, freedom, [and] power" have all been lost. This is a large indictment, and it is presented in terms that are themselves for the most part quite abstract or general. The rhetoric of this poem is far from the specific and detailed images and narrative of a single event offered by Frost. But Frost's poem dealt with the cosmos via the microcosmos. Wordsworth's is limited to England, though we are at liberty to measure our own situation against his.

His ruling metaphor is the swamp or "fen / Of stagnant waters" that he claims England has become. And he sees this poet, Milton, as having a voice and a soul strong enough to part these stagnant waters. In particular he sets against that image of the fen, images of star, sea, and heavens. But my rhetorical point is that this is an argument in what Aristotle would call enthymemic form—which means that key elements in the chain of reasoning are assumed or suppressed. We can analyze this process as follows:

(stated) England has degenerated and lost its virtues.
(assumed) This condition can be ameliorated by a soul with a voice.
(stated, metaphorically) The proper soul / voice will be like star, sea, and heavens.
(stated) Milton had such a voice.
(stated conclusion) Milton is needed at this hour.

As you can see, the poem begins with its conclusion—which is not unusual in persuasive discourse. Then follows a chain of argument supporting that conclusion. Looking carefully, we can see that, of the five key pieces in this chain, one is assumed and one is stated only in metaphorical terms. Which does not mean that Wordsworth is wrong, but it does mean that we can see how to make a strong counterargument—by attacking the assumption as invalid, and arguing that no voice could do this job, or rejecting the metaphoric description of Milton's voice. Ezra Pound, for example, characterized Milton's rhetoric as an "abominable dog-biscuit"—which is a long way from sea, star, and heaven. Or one could reject Wordsworth's characterization of England's condition in 1802 as degenerate. Destroy any link in the enthymemic chain and you destroy the argument.

But I don't want to argue with Wordsworth, myself. I think we could use Milton's voice right now, as a matter of fact, if he would speak to us. But I do want to demonstrate that we can use a poem like Wordsworth's very well in the course of discussing how we should argue, how we should reason, and how we should consider a text before giving assent to it. One can, of course, reject the argument and still admire the rhetoric and enjoy the poem. I admire a lot of Saint Paul's rhetoric, but I don't agree with anything he says except that one should "take a little wine" every now and then, as he advised his friend Timothy, in a letter. Taken together, however, I am arguing that poems like these sonnets of Frost and Wordsworth can demonstrate their usefulness very well in the study of rhetoric and composition—and across the whole trivium of logic, rhetoric, and grammar, if it comes to that. To make the most of this usefulness, however, we will have to connect reading and writing more closely, seeing improvement in writing as an end of our studies of texts called "literary." We can, indeed, use poetical texts to help students reason and argue more effectively—and we should be doing just this.

If we look a little deeper into Wordsworth's sonnet, we can see something else as well. His Milton is not only a "star." He is someone who lived an ordinary life, whose heart accepted and performed the "lowliest duties." And it is the combination of his great soul and powerful voice with a heart inspired by "cheerful godliness" that makes the possibility of his return so attractive. We can imagine, I should think, the appeal of someone with this combination of attributes, and can perhaps believe that such a person could make a difference in our world. We might even vote for such a person—or someone we believed was such a person. Still, if we are examining the logic of Wordsworth's argument, we would have to inquire into whether this characterization of Milton is justified.

This would mean, if the poem were under discussion in a writing course, that some investigation of Wordsworth's claim about Milton's life would be in order. What low duties is Wordsworth talking about? And did Milton really undertake any? What sort of life did he have, anyway? In the poem Wordsworth seems to assume that his audience of 1802 would accept such a statement, based on some common notions about the life of the poet. So the interesting question becomes what a literate English person of that era could be expected to know or believe about Milton's life—and what would be the source of such information. These interpretive questions could easily lead to a little research—not only into Milton's life but into writings about Milton's life published before 1802. Taking this poem seriously as an argument, then, can lead a class to all sorts of interesting projects and discussions.

If I were conducting such a class, I would try to lead students to looking at Samuel Johnson's "Life of Milton," a chapter in *Lives of the Poets* which had appeared just twenty years earlier, to see whether it might support Wordsworth's claims. I should add that, if we do look there, we shall see that Johnson speaks of Milton's performing such lowly tasks as teaching boys to read literary works that deal with things in life and nature, including poems like Virgil's *Georgics*, which are about farming. When we look into things, as Frost looked into his little scene, we often find connections, and we seldom escape irony completely. Certainly, I find it ironic that Milton, as a teacher, in some sense anticipated my concerns here, using poetry as if it were a serious kind of discourse and not something airily detached from life. Which is why, no doubt, Wordsworth turned to him in the first place, and why I turned to Frost and Wordsworth, who can both be said to be in the tradition of *The Georgics* to some extent.

Now clearly, if we allow these poems by Frost and Wordsworth to be literature, it is a mistake to call something literature as a way of removing it from serious study as intellectual discourse. Moreover, if this trick can be done with sonnets, I hope you will allow that it can also be done with such loose and baggy monsters as plays and novels. At the simplest level, as we have seen, this literary designation may rule excellent written texts out of consideration in our basic courses in reading, writing, and thinking. And that is one reason why we need to free ourselves from a restricted notion of literature. But there are other reasons, that run in the opposite direction. People on the other side of the great divide between reading and writing are just as likely to use the notion of literature in an exclusive way—and this is just as big a mistake. That is, they will rule out of serious consideration whole categories of texts that fail to meet their own definitions of what is literary.

This sort of exclusion starts with something as venerable as the essay, which took its modern name and form around the time of Shakespeare. If I may descend to personal anecdote again, I want to tell you about another anthology in which I was involved, called *Elements of Literature*, which included plays, stories, and poems. The trouble started when we proposed to include the essay as a fourth literary mode alongside of the three that everyone acknowledged to be literary. This was resisted by our publisher and by some of our users as well—which is more serious, since they are the ones who order the book for their courses—resisted because essays were not "literature." The supposed distinction between texts that are allowed to be "literature" and those that are not can be applied from either side of this imaginary gap. The essay, when seen from the literary side of the gap, is considered insufficiently creative, and the poem, when seen from the compositional side, is considered insufficiently practical. But most of the texts that matter to us combine these qualities, offering us food for thought presented with formal elegance and power.

This is why I, and the sort of people who have joined me in producing such textbooks, reject the narrow notion that would deny to anything called literature a place in the world of work and public events, along with the other notion that restricts literature to poetry, drama, and fiction. A very good poet said that "poetry makes nothing happen," but this was in a moment of disgust with his own failure to change the world with his poems. Auden, who said this in an elegy for W. B. Yeats, was premature in taking this stand. His poems have not changed the world politically, as he might have wished, but they have made a cultural difference, especially in the area of gender studies. Modernist writers, paradoxically, often wanted their works to change the world, but also wanted them free of that world's messiness. Yeats himself felt guilty about the political effects of his own writing, and famously asked, "Did that play of mine send out / Certain men the English shot?" But he didn't deny the effect. The editorial groups in which I have been involved were made up of individuals who all believed that admirable writing can be found in many sorts of texts, and that the most admirable writing often does real work in the actual world. We would not deny that certain kinds of texts, like instructions, are usually very low on the literary scale, but we all believe that there is a scale, and that there are poems, plays, stories, and expository texts all along that scale. This scale is a measure of a quality we may call "literariness" (which I would define as a combination of textual pleasure and power), but it is neither easy nor right to draw a line across the scale at some point and call everything on one side of the line literature. Nor is it right to insist that some particular formal quality—like the sonnet form—or some particular sort of content—like the social condition of England—will be sufficient to assign any text a particular place on the scale.

Having considered two poems that I believe should not be limited by inclusion within a restricted notion of literature, I would now like to offer examples of two texts that are not usually classed as literary but have a strong claim to literariness. We can begin with a brief passage from an ancient Greek prose text (which I present here transliterated, with the continuous prose text broken into syntactic units of one line each).

> *Ton kalon agona egonismai*
> *Ton dromon teteleka*
> *Ten pistin tetereka*

Let us consider the sound of it first. This text has a rhythm and a sonic pattern that is not quite rhyme but not far from it either. It is familiar to us in various English versions that go something like this:

> I have fought the good fight; I have stayed the course; I have kept the faith.

If we make a close translation, we get something like this:

> The good fight I have fought
> The course I have finished
> The faith I have kept

What kind of text is this? It is from a letter—a letter from one man to another, in which the writer is speaking of his life's work, which he feels is coming to an end. The writer is known to us as Saint Paul, and the recipient of this epistle is his friend Timothy (2 Timothy 4:7). They corresponded in Greek, which was the lingua franca of the Mediterranean world at that time, though other languages, including Latin, were widely used as well. And, if there is one thing certain about this Paul, it is that he had a feel for the Greek language and probably had rhetorical training in that language. The rhythms, as I have suggested, are powerful and insistent in this passage. But let us look more closely at the words themselves.

Take the first line. The primary meaning of *kalon* is beautiful, often extended to goodness in general. *Agona* means crowd or gathering, especially a crowd gathered to watch a contest such as a race or fight or the Olympic games; hence, it also means contest or struggle. *Egonismai* or *agonizmai* refers to contending for a prize, in oratory, on the stage, or in public games. The first line or clause in this expression, then, has to do with public performance, with a contest for a prize, and with doing this beautifully. It does not mention winning. Rather, it seems to be about what Ernest Hemingway called "grace under pressure," which may be the best one can do in certain circumstances. What interests me here is the linking of physical and verbal struggle with the combination of beauty and goodness, and the strong indication that all this has taken place in a large public arena.

In the second line, the key words are *dromon* and *teteleka*. *Dromon* refers to running and especially to running in an arena. A hippodrome is where horses run. And *teteleka* means to complete, to fulfill, and, generally, to perform. Once again, in this line, we have a mixture of references to public athletic events, to performance, but this time the athletic metaphor requires completion for this to be a good or beautiful performance. Once again, however, victory is not mentioned. This is about finishing a race, not about winning one, about staying the course. The last line follows this process to its conclusion, with *tetereka*, I have watched over, guarded, or kept, and *pistin*, the faith, trust, or, in rhetoric, the proof. In other contexts Paul speaks about winning such contests, but it is clear, in any case, that metaphors of racing were often in his mind.

This is a discourse about religious faith, to be sure. Let us put the text in its larger context, in the King James Version:

> I charge thee therefore before God, and the Lord Jesus Christ, who shall judge the quick and the dead at his appearing and his kingdom; Preach the word; be instant in season, out of season; reprove, rebuke, exhort with all longsuffering and doctrine. For the time will come when they will not endure sound doctrine; but after their own lusts shall they heap to themselves teachers, having itching ears; And they shall turn away their ears from the truth, and shall be turned unto fables. But watch thou in all things, endure afflictions, do the work of an evangelist, make full proof of thy ministry. For I am now ready to be offered, and the time of my departure is at hand. I have fought a good fight, I have finished my course, I have kept the faith.

Paul is telling Timothy what he is going to have to deal with as a minister to a flock that will constantly need shepherding. Because they have "itching ears" they will turn away from the truth to be scratched by fables. And Timothy must use all the rhetorical tricks in his bag to counter these fabulous lures. As Paul says, "reprove, rebuke, exhort with all longsuffering and doctrine." I like the "long-suffering" in particular, because it suggests Paul's own method. If doctrine won't do it, perhaps enacting the minister's own suffering will move them. It is not enough to "endure inflictions," whether from the Romans or from one's own flock, one must enact those inflictions so that the flock will be moved by the long-suffering of the minister. This, among other things, is included in that advice to "make full proof of thy ministry." And it is only after this advice, that Paul reminds Timothy that the baton is being passed to him for the next lap of this race, which will end only when the Judge appears to impose his kingdom.

Paul's words, in this passage, have been quoted or simply plagiarized for centuries, and it is still going on. That mixture of religion and athleticism, with a touch of agony thrown in, still proves irresistible to our politicians and to our preachers—if it is possible to make such a distinction anymore. And these words do work in the world. They move people. They influence elections. They are functional. They are also beautiful—by which I mean that they are compelling for the way that they juggle sounds and meanings so as to be at once powerful and direct, on the one hand, and subtle and complex, on the other. Hearing them used now, we are likely to be moved by them without registering consciously the combination of rhythms and figures of speech that gives them their power. Approaching them as literature should enable us to see that Paul is telling a fable against fables, using the resources of literature and rhetoric against the literary and rhetorical tricks that will scratch the itching ears of Timothy's flock. In short, he knew, himself, how to scratch that itch for textual pleasure that he deplored. And that textual power of his is what has moved his writing to such a central place in Christianity. He got there the old-fashioned way. He earned it—with rhetoric.

My point here is that Paul's epistles would normally be excluded from a course in literature and, indeed, from the literary canon as a whole—perhaps because he is in another canon. If his words are simply true—gospel, as we say—then they can't be literature. And, conversely, if something is literature, it can't be true. Such notions make me wish to follow Paul's advice and "reprove, rebuke, exhort with all longsuffering and doctrine." Many English teachers seem to believe that texts must belong to the category Paul called "fables" to be literary. That is part of our problem, because it limits what we teach and how we teach it. I shall be arguing that we need to pay much more attention to texts often thought of as "sacred," precisely because they are powerful shapers of our values and our lives. But let us consider one more example of a work that falls outside of our narrow definition of literature but is nevertheless a text of power and beauty. This one comes from a work of historical journalism:

> Were I to go down into the market-place, armed with the powers of witchcraft, and take a peasant by the shoulders and whisper to him, "In your lifetime, have you known peace?" wait for his answer, shake his shoulders and transform him into his father, and ask him the same question, and transform him in turn into his father, I would never hear the word "Yes," if I carried my questioning of the dead back for a thousand years. I would always hear, "No, there was prison, there was torture, there was violent death."

These words were written by Rebecca West, in her book about traveling in Yugoslavia just before World War II, *Black Lamb and Grey Falcon*. This is journalism, then, but it is strongly marked by the quality of literariness. In the previous example, the rhythms and metaphorical play of Paul's language lifted it to the level of memorability, making his words so powerful that they have continued to echo down the centuries. In this case something different is going on. The words themselves are not so memorable, I would say, but the scene and the images are. West as a witch in a market-place, shaking a peasant by the shoulders, whispering a question, and transforming him into his father and on back through the generations—this is an image difficult to forget. And there is a powerful truth in what she is saying, expressed through the fiction of the witch in the marketplace and the simple rhythms of the reply, "there was prison, there was torture, there was violent death." And the truth is that these things still are with us, and closer to us than ever. She could shake one of us and get the same reply.

West wrote fiction, too, but I doubt if any of her novels or stories is more literary than *Black Lamb and Grey Falcon*, in which she was testifying, bearing witness to places she had visited, people she had talked to, and things she had seen. But not many journalists or writers of contemporary history would imagine themselves as witches to bring home the lessons they had learned. Nor could many of them represent it so well if they tried to do so. It is important that the witch should shake the peasant and whisper her question, "have you known peace?" which is a very whisperable phrase, dominated by the long vowel and that sinister sibilant in the final word. All good fantasy is realistic in its treatment of the supernatural, and this fantastic moment is given that quality by its location in a marketplace, and by the specificity of the witch's grip on the peasant's shoulders, as well as by the whisper itself.

Among many other things, West's great book is a defense of art, and of Mozart and Jane Austen in particular. Thinking of Susanna's song in the last act of Mozart's *Marriage of Figaro*, "Deh vieni, non tardar" (O, come, don't delay), during the bombing of London, West asks herself, "Can you say that a bomb which might have blown you to smithereens matters less than a song supposed to be sung by a lady's maid, who, however, never existed, when waiting for the embraces of a valet, who, also, never existed?" And her answer is simply, "Yes." For those who love art and music, the bombs intensify their delight in those things. I cannot repeat here West's full discussion of the song Mozart gave this lady's maid, but part of her argument is that the composer had captured "in a melody the tones of a human voice speaking out of tender and protective love," and that we need to hear such things more than ever when such voices seem to be drowned out by bombs and the cries of victims. This discussion of the usefulness of Mozart's song is part of a larger consideration of art and its functions that runs from the first pages of West's book to the last—which amounts to well over a thousand pages of text. "These days," she says, "have given us a chance to test the artistic process, and judge whether it is a tool that does honest work or whether it simply makes toys for the childish." And while admitting that, "[p]erhaps half the total artistic activity of man has been counterfeit," she still argues that art is a "reliving of experience," that it can help each of us to "understand what my life means."

Now, part of what I have said here can be seen as an attempt to answer West's question about whether literature does "honest work," by showing that two very literary sonnets do indeed discuss serious questions that connect to the worlds of politics and religion. I have also tried to show that texts like those of Paul and Rebecca West, which come from those excluded worlds of religion and politics, may nevertheless be strongly marked with qualities we recognize as literary. In the rest of this book I hope to show that we have much to gain by moving from the limiting notion of literature to the more inclusive concept of textuality—a move which I believe can help restore to English studies some of the power and pleasure that they have lost in recent years.

CHAPTER THREE

Textuality and the Teaching of Reading

ONE PROBLEM WITH THE RESTRICTED NOTION OF LITERATURE is that you can read it but you can't write it. And that restriction has led to the separation of the study of reading/literature in our English departments from the study of writing/composition, which has become a hierarchical structure with mainly untenured adjuncts at the bottom, teaching writing, and tenured or tenurable faculty at the top, teaching literature. To this has been added the further split between those kinds of writing that can be designated as "creative" and those that cannot. The creative sorts of writing aspire to the condition of literature but cannot claim it. But the restricted notion of literature drives the claim to creativity. We now have programs claiming creative status for certain sorts of writing not included in the restricted notion of literature, like the personal essay. This division and confusion is one part of the problem. Another part of the problem is that our notion of literature is too tightly tied to the book, so that it excludes work in other print media (like magazines and newspapers) and work in the audiovisual media that dominate our culture. Furthermore, this notion is tied to a narrow view of what makes a text creative or literary, which keeps the most powerful religious and political texts out of our classrooms, along with the most powerful audiovisual texts. And finally, the restricted notion of literature with its narrow view of the creative imagination prevents us from demonstrating in our classrooms the relevance of the texts we cherish to the actual lives of our students.

To solve these problems we need to redefine English as the study of textuality rather than literature. Such a redefinition has a number of aspects, but it begins with the recognition that English is all about teaching—not research—and that this teaching has two main branches: reading and writing. That is, the business of English departments is to help students improve as readers and writers, to become better producers and consumers of verbal texts. That's all there is to it. It is a humble business, but it is the only justification for the existence of these departments in this fallen world. And it is not easy to do it well. In this book I intend to concentrate on the reading side of the problem: what sorts of texts should be taught and how they should be approached. But first I need to say a few words about the relationship of writing and reading instruction.

Disagree

When I taught at the University of Iowa, I once proposed, in an English Department meeting, that all PhD candidates in English should take a course in the Writers' Workshop, learning to write in the genre they were studying—because this experience would make them better readers of those texts. This proposal was not approved. The creative writers understood the reasoning, but the literary critics did not—or professed not to. MFA candidates often took courses in literature—and made use of them, as John Gardner made use of the course in Old English that he took while at Iowa, which bore fruit later in his novel *Grendel*—but this was a one-way street.

In those same years at Iowa, I frequently team-taught a multi-credit undergraduate course in English from the Renaissance to the nineteenth century, in which students were asked to perform scenes from every play we read, from Shakespeare to Shaw and Wilde. The purpose of this was to put them on the creative side of the process, as a way of helping them become better critics. One function of textuality is to bridge the gap between production and consumption: to see reading as involving an imaginative act of recreating the original situation of a text—the people who produced it and those who were being addressed by it. Bridging this gap also involves going in the other direction, seeing every text as a response to others, a kind of reading. In that Iowa course, students also were asked to write in the form of the texts we were reading: to produce a Spenserian stanza on some chosen subject, for example, or a Baconian essay. This kind of work is part of the move from reaction to interpretation, which I shall describe more fully below. In an effort to bring reading and writing together, some colleagues and I produced a textbook called *Text Book*, which featured assignments that combined critical and creative thinking and writing. I have used this book myself in a course called "Textuality," but I am using the term here in a larger sense.

As I see it, textuality has two aspects. One is the broadening of the objects we study and teach to include all the media and modes of expression. All the kinds of texts students regularly encounter in their lives should be studied in this field. And they should also be encouraged to expand their interests to include certain texts they do not normally see—like opera. Expanding the range of texts is one aspect of studies in textuality. The other, as I have already indicated, has to do with changing the way we look at texts to combine the perspectives of creator and consumer, writer and reader. Both of these aspects of textuality have to do with helping students open their minds and expand their vision of how texts work and what they do. The larger goal of textuality is the opening of a wider world of culture for students, which means, to begin with, that teachers must know some things that students do not know. But it also means more than that. It means that teachers must be able to devise pathways into that wider world that will make it engaging and accessible. We should know by now that it is not enough just to throw great books at students and say, "Catch!" The basic purpose of humanistic education is to give students perspectives on their own cultural situation, opening the past so that they can connect it to the present.

There is a great teaching scene in John Ford's Western film *The Man Who Shot Liberty Valance*, in which a lawyer-turned-reading-teacher (Ransom Stoddard, played by James Stewart) is educating illiterate students—old and young, white, black, and Latino—in the town of Shinbone. He uses two texts: the Declaration of Independence and a current issue of the *Shinbone Star*, the local newspaper. And he connects both texts to the lives of all his students. The habitually drunken editor of that newspaper, by the way, is always quoting or paraphrasing Shakespeare, though only moviegoers with a certain amount of cultural background will recognize the source of his eloquence.

What do Shakespeare, the Declaration of Independence, and the *Shinbone Star* have in common? They are all alive, in the culture of the film world, and, if you substitute any local paper for the *Star*, in our own world as well. They are texts that matter, though they matter in different ways. And they come to us from different places in history and through different media. Shakespeare's plays come from an oral culture, taking their existence in the form of dramatic production, surviving in print almost by accident. Jefferson's document, written with the help of a committee in Philadelphia, comes from an Enlightenment culture, strongly influenced by French political thought, and was first published as a printed broadside and read aloud in village squares throughout the colonies. The local newspaper, also from a print culture, represents yet another medium, the periodical. But all three of these cultural texts, we must remember, are coming to us now through the medium of film—one of the great Western films that has added to our own stock of memorable scenes and words, including those of a later editor of the *Shinbone Star*, who refuses to print Stoddard's true version of history, saying, "This is the West, sir. When the legend becomes fact, print the legend."

Culture, of course, is a blend of fact and legend, but it is powerful, and we are in its grip. We must start from where we are, which means that we must begin by recognizing and accepting our situation. As I see it, most English teachers are in a world where people want from them those things they consider most trivial and annoying: instruction in the basic functions of language. And teachers are also in a world where the things they most value, the masterpieces of English literature, have lost much of their appeal and interest. To put things bluntly, they want to sell what most of their potential customers do not want to buy, and those customers want to buy what English teachers can't be bothered to sell. The only solution to this situation that I can see is to address both of these issues directly. That is, we must find ways to make what students actually want and need more rewarding for their teachers, and we must find ways of making what teachers wish to teach more interesting and useful for those who may come to them for instruction. The solution, in my view, is to put these two aspects of English education back together. That is, teachers must not simply advise students how to consume texts but help them to understand how these texts were constructed in the first place. The study of textuality involves looking at works that function powerfully in our world, and considering both what they mean and how they mean. And here I will take my point of departure from the young Ransom Stoddard rather than from the editor who rejected the factual version of the shooting of Liberty Valance in favor of the fictional one.

Stoddard chose texts that connected directly to the lives of his students. Neither the *Shinbone Star* nor the Declaration of Independence would count as literature in the world of English studies which has fallen around us. And that is one thing English teachers need to change if they are to find their way after the fall. Political and religious texts must be in English courses along with the customary literary genres, and so must works of journalism. As I understand it, this means going beyond tinkering with the syllabus. I believe English faculties must reorient their entire perspective on the present and the past, and the key to that reorientation lies in a room right next to the space where Ransom Stoddard held his little class in that memorable film. In that room are a printing press and the type used to set the *Shinbone Star*. Our modern era begins with the invention of the printing press in the fifteenth century. And the key to reorienting English studies lies in the notion of print as a medium of communication that is connected to the audiovisual and digital media that now dominate our culture. Studies of print culture and the history of the book have begun to flourish lately, and they can help indicate where we must go, but they often take their point of departure from the difference between print and the later media. I would argue, on the other hand, that it is even more important to recognize connections between this earlier world and our own—and the connections are there, if we will look for them.

One such connection involves *The Man Who Shot Liberty Valance* itself. This text did not begin as a movie, but as a short story in *Cosmopolitan* magazine. The author, Dorothy Marie Johnson, was from Montana, and had returned there after working on magazines in New York for fifteen years. She wrote a series of stories in the late 1940s and early 1950s, collected as *Indian Country* in 1953. Two of these stories, "The Man Who Shot Liberty Valance" and "A Man Called Horse," were made into movies. But there is more to the story than that. There are interesting differences between Johnson's story and the film based on it, though the character called Ranse teaches English in both versions. In the short story, however, he woos Hallie by quoting Shakespeare's sonnets to her—and he tells no one the truth about who shot Valance. When *Indian Country* was released in paperback it was clearly seen as something to be used in schools, and it came with "A Note to Teachers and Parents" written by Richard Tyre, who was the chairman of English at the Germantown Friends School. Tyre explained the educational value of the book, which, he said, "gives the student or searcher after first-rate western stories the very rare experience of being in the log cabin with the homesteader, wanting to kill murdering Indians; while realizing that in our Westward Movement we destroyed an Indian civilization that had profound religious, moral, and ethical traditions." Tyre also provided brief suggestions for teaching the stories, including this one about "Liberty Valance": "*The Man Who Shot Liberty Valance* is perfect for a Hollywood Western and it would make a fine class exercise to turn it into one."

That, of course, is exactly what happened, though it was done not by a class of high school students but by the great master of Westerns, John Ford. Ford was aided in this effort by two screenwriters who did an excellent job of conversion from one medium to another, enriching it, for example, by adding episodes like the senator's telling of the truth to the journalist who refuses to print it. But the tale did not end there. One of the authors of the screenplay was John Warner Bellah, whose stories were made into a number of films by Ford, including *Fort Apache*, *She Wore a Yellow Ribbon*, and *Rio Grande*. Bellah also wrote a novelization of *The Man Who Shot Liberty Valance*, leaving us, then, with a story that had multiple texts and multiple authors. The paperback of Johnson's *Indian Country* also has a preface by Jack Warner, whose novel *Shane* was turned into a screenplay by A. B. Guthrie Jr. and became an Oscar-winning film. In his short foreword to Johnson's book, Warner praised her stories as works that "gave a new dimension to what we now call the American heritage. They face forward. They affirm life. They assert that man, in defeat as in victory, can be equal to his fate." One can hear anticipations of William Faulkner's Nobel Prize speech in these words. But the point we need to register is how texts in various media, and their authors, move from one world to another, one medium to another, making a culture that is interesting—and teachable—on many levels.

Ford's film is an excellent example of textuality at work, because it directs our attention to both sacred and profane verbal texts, reminding us, among other things, that we cannot count on the media to tell us the truth—that all texts require interpretation and a critical response. *The Man Who Shot Liberty Valance* is one of the first films to show us two versions of the same event—a false one (the legend) followed by a true one (the fact)—a device now commonplace on shows like *CSI*. And the theme of truth versus falsehood runs through the entire text. The *Shinbone Star* dares to print the truth about the social and political situation in the territory, and the editor is badly beaten and his office wrecked because of this. Because the newspaper prints the facts, Ransom Stoddard picks it up and takes it into his classroom for study. All of which makes the irony of the paper's later acquiescence into "legend" more disturbing. The First Amendment to the Constitution protected the freedom of the press because the founders thought it essential to the workings of government in a republic. But the press does not always live up to the high standard that justifies its freedom. This film pays major attention to the political process—the registration of voters, the debate over statehood, the interests of small farmers versus large ranchers. And behind this is the larger historical process, which situates the frontier rule of the gun versus the rule of law. Stoddard represents the rule of the law, with his law books, his drive to register voters, his teaching of the basic political texts of the country. Liberty Valance is an outlaw, representing raw power at its ugliest. And Tom Doniphan both argues and demonstrates that the law needs the gun to back it up.

The sheriff of Shinbone, played superbly by Andy Devine, is supposed to represent the law, but he is a coward, who hides when Valance is in town and resists legal arguments calling for this thug's arrest. He is also a glutton and a moocher, chomping down steaks on credit at the town's restaurant. And he is a lecher of sorts, having begotten a large brood of children on his Latina wife. This is the reality of law in Shinbone—a sheriff locked up in his own jail by Valance and his men who make a mockery of law and justice. Stoddard, the young man from the East, represents the ideal of the law. He is, in fact, too idealistic to survive without help in that world. But he attracts the attention of Hallie, the illiterate daughter of the restaurant's owners and draws her away from Tom Doniphan, who has been planning to marry her but hadn't yet got around to proposing when Stoddard arrived in town. Doniphan, played very well by John Wayne, sees Hallie's affections shifting to Stoddard, but tries to advise him and teach him the ways of the frontier, because his death would be painful to Hallie. And finally, in the shootout between Stoddard and Valance, when Stoddard is clearly going to be killed, Doniphan shoots Valance with a rifle while hidden across the road, saving the wounded Stoddard's life and losing Hallie to him as a result.

The film begins with the return of Senator Stoddard and his wife to Shinbone for the funeral of the now unknown Doniphan. There, Stoddard tells the editor of the paper the true story of the shooting, while Hallie goes and gets a cactus flower to put on Doniphan's coffin. And in this true story Stoddard explains not only that Doniphan shot Valance but that he told Stoddard about it in time for him to free himself from the guilt he felt for having killed another person—no matter how deserving—and to go on to lead the fight for statehood and become governor, ambassador, and senator in a long career. This film, like *Casablanca*, was a studio production, which meant that there was a large supply of excellent actors and actresses to take large parts and small ones, to make these characters live, act, and die before our eyes. And, like *Casablanca*, it was shot in black and white, which, paradoxically, gives it an aura of authenticity and historicity that films in the colors of the real world can hardly match. For us, however, this lack of color can be seen as an indication of artifice. This whole film, including the "true" story, is a legend, a fiction, a text.

The film is full of memorable touches, like a speech against statehood splendidly hammed up by John Carradine, and the entry of a cowboy on horseback riding up onto the stage at the statehood meeting and back down out the door, to demonstrate the frontier spirit that was resisting absorption by a government that had declared its independence so long ago and recently fought to preserve its union. The resistance to statehood was real, powerful, and doomed, because history was on the other side. But history did not just happen. People fought and died for it, as this film reminds us. Another memorable touch is the performance of the sheriff's oldest daughter in the schoolroom. She is a bright young woman, too bright in fact, and wants to answer all the questions, so that Stoddard has to urge her to let the others answer some. Unlike many Westerns, including some very good ones, this one is not about the landscape, it is about the social and political side of our history, and there is every reason why it should be studied and taught in our classrooms. Above all, students should be investigating the ways in which a text like this evolved from a relatively simple short story to be enriched by elaboration of the plot, as well as by the performance of actors, and the camera and editing work that created the final cinematic text.

Much of the material we have just considered was not in the original story, which should definitely be made available in the classroom so that the evolution of a complex text like this film can be explored in such a way as to heighten the pleasure and increase the understanding of those who are studying it. Every change in event or character is worth exploring, though I do not wish to stop and do that now. If I were teaching this film, however, I would invite students to start by making a list of all the additions, subtractions, and modifications worked by the makers of the film upon Dorothy Johnson's original text. Once we have noted all these, we are in a position to explore the reasons for them and to evaluate critically every change from the original story to the film as we have it. Every text owes something to others that have preceded it, and adds something of its own, but a case like this one makes that process especially clear and allows us to understand the final result more fully and to enjoy it more thoroughly as well. And that is one justification for studies in textuality.

By giving the world of journalism such prominence, this film can serve as a reminder of the importance of all those journalistic texts usually left out of the English curriculum, though they have a long history in our culture. Periodicals began to take a recognizable form in the seventeenth century and became regularized in English in the eighteenth. They are printed texts that appear at intervals, often regular intervals, though not always, and they have lives that can be as short as one or two issues or as long as a century or more. They appear with frequencies ranging from daily to annually, and some are quite irregular. In this way they are the predecessors of our television shows. Perhaps the most important connection between a printed periodical and a regular television show lies in their shared use of advertising. We sometimes forget how old advertising is. When one of Shakespeare's characters wonders "if it be true that good wine needs no bush," she is talking about the foliage hung outside tavern doors to advertise the good cheer within. Signs have been with us for quite a while. But printed advertising takes a recognizable form with the coming of periodicals. There were regular advertisements, for example, in the *Spectator*, three centuries ago, though most students of English are unaware of that because the ads have been suppressed in reprints of the original texts.

It is ironic, to be sure, that these ads have now become at least as interesting as many of the essays of Addison and Steele which they originally accompanied. Advertising becomes a pleasure for us as it loses its direct connection with consumption and simply offers us a window into its world. When Ezra Pound, in 1917, sought to understand what he called the "Contemporary Mentality" of Britain, he turned to the magazines and tried to explore all the social levels reached by them in a series of twenty articles he wrote for the *New Age*. When he found ads for the treatment of lice in children's hair, he felt he had descended far enough, having reached what he called a "verminous level." The advertisements in old magazines are not literature, to be sure, but they are rhetoric, and they offer us culture in the raw, waiting to be interpreted and understood. Our present cultural saturation in advertising has equipped teachers—and their students—to approach the advertising of the past with critical sophistication, and the fact that this advertising is indeed from the past and puts no direct consumptive pressure on us, means that we can take an aesthetic pleasure in its rhetorical displays, as well as a historical interest in the habits of consumers. The culture of the past is more alive in its magazines than in any other textual form, because it is all there, the art and the lice, the truth and the lies.

Until very recently it was impossible to teach using the periodicals of the past because we could not put them in the hands of students. But the availability of digital editions has changed all that. These editions, to be sure, are of varying quality, and there is much work to be done to provide just what we need—especially since it has been a regular practice in our libraries to discard the advertising pages when periodicals are bound and entered into their permanent collections. And the great commercial digitizers of our time are just scanning and reproducing those impoverished bound copies of the originals. There is archival work to be done, and editorial work to be done, before the best pedagogical work may be done. And this is real work, scholarship that is needed and justified by its contribution to teaching and learning. We also need to recognize that the period of modernism is crucial in our cultural history, because it is the moment of transition to our own world. In the 1890s advertising came to dominate the world of magazines, as publishers learned that they could lower their price per issue, increase circulation, and still profit through the advertising revenue generated by their large circulations. The "little magazines" of modernism arose in reaction to this move toward mass circulation in the larger magazines, which made the popular magazines less open to experimental and challenging texts. Both these phenomena began in the 1890s and reached a peak in the first decades of the twentieth century. The decline of the popular magazines like *Colliers*, *Life*, and *Look*, was caused by the way that audiences and advertising revenue migrated to television after World War II.

We can use the resources of the audiovisual media and digital technology as windows into the cultural past, and we can emphasize the ways in which the print media of that past connect to the newer modes of textual production. The actress Emma Thompson won an Oscar for her screenplay of Jane Austen's *Sense and Sensibility*, and she wrote a very good book about the filming of the movie itself, in which she played a role. With a class, one could start with the film, then read Thompson's book, and finally read Jane Austen, who can certainly hold her own. But a discussion based on all three texts will enable students to consider the ways in which all three were composed and produced, and the worlds from which they emerged. Thompson studied English at Newnham College, Cambridge, and she has used her education well, becoming the only person to win Oscars for both acting and writing. Clearly, Jane Austen interested her, to the point where she adapted Austen's novel for the medium of film and then wrote about the filming in the print medium, while acting in the film she had written. This situation can enable us to consider the possibilities of the different media, and the things that persist in the movement from one to another.

Similar things can be done with other important texts in our culture. The fifteen episodes of the BBC video of *Bleak House* can lead to Dickens's novel and its serial publication, where the episodes of the novel were embedded in advertisements like the one that proclaims "Woe to the inhabitants of the Bleak House if he is not armed with the weapons of an OVERCOAT and a

SUIT OF FASHIONABLE and substantial Clothing, such as can only be obtained at E. MOSES & SON'S Establishments, Aldgate and Minories, New Oxford-street, and Hart-street, London; or 36, Fargate, Sheffield, or 19, Bridge-street, Bradford, Yorkshire." Such advertising can help our students make the connection between our world and that world of Dickens—a world which can often seem so strangely different when encountered via the screen or printed book. And this connection can lead to others as they recognize that the problems of poverty and disease so visible in the Dickens texts are still with us, that lawyers are still lawyers, and doctors, doctors. The writers from the past that we need are the ones who are still talking to us, whether about social problems we recognize, or thoughts and feelings that we still experience in our own lives. Jane Austen and Charles Dickens, different as they are, still speak to us now.

As students come to see the connections between the past and our present, they will become more interested in the differences as well. To understand our world we need to see it from other perspectives. Consider, for example, the *Spectator* No. 75, from three centuries ago. In it we will find among the advertisements one for "An Incomparable Pleasant Tincture to restore the sense of smelling, tho' lost for many years. A few Drops of which being snuffed up the Nose, infallibly Cures those who have lost their Smell, let it proceed from what Cause soever." This miracle brew is offered for sale at "Mr. Payne's Toyshop at the Angel and Crown in St. Paul's Church Yard near Cheapside with Directions" (http://meta.montclair.edu/spectator). The loss of this sense is a recognized ailment in our time (anosmia), with many possible causes including age and drugs, but in this case we must conclude that the era of snuff-taking generated an unusual demand for the restoration of the sense of smell. Students will have no trouble connecting this ad to contemporary nostrums for other ailments, even as they become aware of the cultural peculiarities that make this "Pleasant

Tincture" so appropriate to that distant past. Such ads can make the past real for students, and therefore really engaging.

As one writer observed, in his book on the most popular monthly magazine in Britain in the early twentieth century,

> *The Strand Magazine* advertisements filled an average of a hundred pages a month, representing more than two hundred and fifty advertisers. They provided it with an envied revenue in its heyday. They indexed the domestic and social life of its readers with something like encyclopedic completeness. We become acquainted with the preferences, prejudices, habits, and conventions of a wide section of society. A sociologist might discover more about the period from those back and front pages of *The Strand* than from the articles and stories between.
>
> We follow the readers' evolving tastes in furnishings, fabrics, clothes, wallpapers, carpets, perambulators, kitchen ware. We see the holiday resorts bidding for their favours. We see the cars they coveted. We are reminded of the cosmetics they used and the patent medicines they took. Their secret dreams are laid bare to us.

Writing half a century ago, this former editor of the *Strand Magazine* captured perfectly the fascination of the advertising in the popular magazines of the modernist period, but what he said is just as true of the two centuries before the *Strand* appeared. It is what the ads tell us about the lives of others that make them so compelling for us now.

Cultural studies have actually been a part of the English curriculum for a while now. I am suggesting that English departments move these studies to the center of the historical dimension of their enterprise, using the connections between contemporary audiovisual media and the earlier print media as a way into our cultural past. This action will also mean historicizing cultural studies, which have tended to be contemporary in their focus. Political history is properly the province of historians, but cultural history is something English teachers share with them and need to claim as part of their field of study and teaching. If English teachers can accept the responsibility to teach all the aspects of textuality—the production, consumption, and history of texts in English—we will have a curriculum that can be competitive in an academic world in which the humanities have been marginalized.

In what follows in this book I take up some of these issues and pursue them to greater depths, concluding with some attempts to illustrate the kind of cultural work I think we should be doing, using the full range of texts available to us in the realm of textuality. For us, of course, textuality begins with the power of words. The importance of this power was illustrated vividly by J. R. Clynes, a British Labour Party Member of Parliament of the early twentieth century, who wrote in his memoirs about being paid three pence a week to read the newspapers to a few blind men in the 1870s:

> Reading aloud was a joy to me. Some of the articles I read from the local Oldham papers of the time must have been pretty poor stuff I suppose, but they went to my head like wine. . . . Then I began to feel the power of words, that strange magic which can excite multitudes to glory, sacrifice or shame. As blindly as my blind hearers, I began to conceive that these words that I loved were more than pretty playthings: they were mighty levers whereby the power of the whole world could be more evenly and fairly distributed for the benefit of my kind.

Textuality begins with the power of words and the pleasures conferred by that power. But it extends to the textual powers and pleasures of other media as well. And that is what English teachers need to study and teach to those who come to them as students, seeking access to those powers and pleasures. The qualities we have thought of as literary are a part—a vital part—of textuality, but they are not the whole of it, and the whole of it should be our focus in the future. Visual signs as well as verbal, oral language as well as written, all the media, starting with books and other printed texts but not ending there, must be our study in the future. Nor should we confine ourselves too strictly to the English language. Textuality is not insular. Although the way back to the paradise. of literature is barred by history and technology, we can save what we love about literature if we recognize the role of language in all the forms and media of textuality.

Lewis and Short's *Latin Dictionary* informs us that our English word *text* comes from the Latin verb *texere*, which means specifically "to weave," and, by extension, "to join or fit together anything; to plait, braid, interweave, interlace; to construct, make, fabricate, build." From *texere* also comes *textum*, "that which is woven, a web . . . that which is plaited, braided, or fitted together," and, when applied to literary composition, "tissue, texture, style." But the connection between textuality and weaving will take us to other places if we follow that thread. In England and Scotland the revolt against clerical control of the biblical texts in the sixteenth and seventeenth centuries was, in fact, led by the weavers in the North of England and the Scottish lowlands, as Jonathan Rose has demonstrated convincingly:

> "There seems to have been a subtle association between weaving and Radicalism in Scotland," noted Clydeside militant David Kirkwood (b. 1872), citing his own great-grandfather as an example. "It may be that these men and women, weaving patterns of cloth, wove at the same time patterns of life. Or it may be that the work, although intricate, became automatic and allowed the mind to browse in the meadows of thought. Did not David Livingstone learn Latin from a text-book propped up in front of him as he wove the cloth?"

These literate men and women read the English Bible and made their own interpretations of it, despite formidable opposition from clerics intent on maintaining their monopoly of the sacred texts. The very translations that they read had been fiercely opposed and the translators persecuted as well by that clerical monopoly. A restricted canon and a limited set of official interpreters have always been in opposition to a wide circulation of texts and interpretations. But the image of a weaver weaving with a "text-book" in front of him should remind us of what textuality is all about: patterns of cloth and patterns of life indeed.

I have been advocating the extension of the curriculum, which I believe should go all the way from the Ten Commandments to advertisements, but I also believe that English teachers should reconsider how they approach such fundamentals as reading itself. To that end I suggest that they, and their students, consider three levels or phases in reading a text.

1. Reaction—a personal response to the text. What does the text mean to the reader? Does the reader like the text or not, and why? This part of the process is crucial, because it makes explicit the reader's original impression, which can then be distinguished from the result of a more deliberate act of interpretation. That is why classroom discussion should begin not with some sophisticated question to which the teacher knows the right answer, but with such simple questions as "Did you like it or not—and why?" and "What does it mean to you?" before moving on to less personal responses.

2. Interpretation—an attempt to see how a text was constructed and to recover the emotional and intellectual intentions of the maker(s) of the text (which may require historical or biographical background). This also requires consideration of the original audience. Quite simply, there can be no meaning without an intention to mean, either our own or another's.

Interpretation, as I am defining it, requires that we look for the intention(s) of the originator(s) of any text without, for the moment, seeking to impose our own meanings. It is a step away from mere reaction toward something more complex. It is also an act that combines research and imagination, since the original producers and consumers of any text are never simply "there" to be discovered, but must be re-created by the interpreter through an act of controlled imagination. This means that no interpretation is ever perfect, though some are clearly better than others.

3. Criticism—a judgment about accepting or rejecting the values embodied in any text and the emotional and intellectual responses it seeks to generate. In this stage of reading we return to our own perspective—but with a difference. This judgment must be informed by interpretation, and it must go beyond the personal toward a critical position that others may be persuaded to accept. It involves "*us*, here, now"—not "*me*, here, now." This is the point at which we judge the value of a text and of the ideas presented in it. But this judgment can be performed in ways that are both serious and playful, ranging from counterarguments to parody and role playing.

These three phases constitute a process of reading that can be enacted in the classroom, starting with the first and ending with the third. The whole process is important, because it addresses a major problem in our culture—the way that naïve readers tend to see their own meanings in every text and fail to recognize other points of view. This means that it is important to make this simple theory of reading explicit in the classroom, so that students will know why they are doing what they are doing. The first phase of reading—reaction—is intended to get that personal response out in the open. And the second phase of reading requires a step away from that first reaction in the direction of the intentions of the originator(s) of the text. The right—and the power—to criticize a text depends on our recognition of a difference between these two perspectives. For texts held to be sacred (the Bill of Rights, the Gospels) the second phase is crucial, while the first might be considered trivial, and the third frowned upon. But, if we are going to teach about seeking the intention behind texts, sacred texts make the best place to start, because everyone agrees that we need to understand them as well as possible.

For such texts, however, the move to criticism is not easy. If God wrote it—or the almost mythical Founding Fathers—we are told we must accept it, not judge it. But the Constitution and the laws of the land do get modified or amended, and even religious texts get reinterpreted over the years. It is also the case that new ones, like the Book of Mormon, appear. There is a lot at stake in the interpretation of sacred texts, which is why we must stop ignoring them in our classrooms. But that is also why they must be handled with care. Depending on the situation, the cautious teacher may wish to use them mainly to teach interpretation—the recovery of original intent—and not make the move to criticism. Even locating the origin of a religious text may be controversial. When was it made? Who wrote it down? What language was used? Who translated it from its original language into our own—and when? There may be debates about these matters, but they should be investigated and discussed. The sacredness of the texts is what energizes their interpretation. If we can bring the full process of reading to our sacred texts—reaction, interpretation, and criticism—we may do more than just energize English teaching. We may help students to a better understanding of their world, and give them the power to change it.

CHAPTER FOUR

Textual Power—Sacred Reading

MANY CULTURES HAVE CREATION NARRATIVES—STORIES OF HOW the world began and human life arose—but one culture's sacred truths about creation are likely to be perceived within another culture as myths and legends, especially if the two cultures have conflicting versions of this "same" event. That is why such texts are especially useful in studying the way that culture itself plays a role in the creation and interpretation of all texts. To understand such texts properly, we need to understand, to the extent that this is possible for us, the circumstances of their origin and the audience originally addressed by them. In a nation like the United States or Canada, Christianity has been the dominant religion since the colonial era, and Christian texts have been considered sacred. But there are many other religions—and many versions of Christianity—operating in North American culture. This is one reason why we should treat all texts held to be sacred with interpretational respect. That is, we must see them as attempts to present a true version of events or a valid way of life, even if they seem to contradict our own views. Which does not mean that we need to believe any of them—even our own. Respect is different from belief.

The texts most cultures consider sacred are those that present crucial truths directly. It is no accident that the most famous sentence in the Declaration of Independence begins with this phrase: "We hold these truths to be self-evident." Texts deemed sacred must be interpreted as directly as possible, as the truth told straight. That belief leads to fundamentalist reading and the notion that texts can—indeed must—be read literally. This becomes complicated when a sacred text like the Bible tells stories that resemble profane narratives, when it seems to present different versions of the same event, or when a person considered divine speaks in parables rather than directly. But most political texts do speak directly—to the people of a particular place and time—whether they take the form of a Magna Carta, a Declaration of Independence, or a Communist Manifesto. Within their own cultural frames of reference they are supposed to lay down the law or tell the truth—or both—which gives them a special kind of textual power. Historical events, like the fall of the Soviet Union, may affect this power for a political text like *The Communist Manifesto*, but every text that has been considered sacred by a significant group of people calls for a very careful kind of reading.

Texts assigned sacred status within a culture are not absolutely different from others, but they do flaunt their claims to truthfulness and lawgiving, so that readers must pay special attention to those claims—understanding them as fully as possible and then examining them with a critical eye to the extent that this is possible. For these are texts that conceal their artfulness and slide over gaps and contradictions—exactly those things the thoughtful reader should investigate.

The Nature of Sacred Texts

Consider, for a moment, a passage from James Joyce's *Ulysses*, in which a speech about the Ten Commandments is being quoted and discussed in a Dublin newspaper office. The speech, originally a response to an argument against reviving the Irish language, pictured Moses in Egypt being addressed by a powerful Egyptian. Here is the part quoted in that Dublin office:

—You pray to a local and obscure idol: our temples, majestic and mysterious, are the abodes of Isis and Osiris, of Horus and Ammon Ra. Yours serfdom, awe and humbleness: ours thunder and the seas. Israel is weak and few are her children: Egypt is an host and terrible are her arms. Vagrants and daylabourers are you called: the world trembles at our name. . . .

—But, ladies and gentlemen, had the youthful Moses listened to and accepted that view of life, had he bowed his head and bowed his will and bowed his spirit before that arrogant admonition he would never have brought the chosen people out of their house of bondage nor followed the pillar of the cloud by day. He would never have spoken with the Eternal amid lightnings on Sinai's mountaintop nor ever have come down with the light of inspiration shining in his countenance and bearing in his arms the tables of the law, graven in the language of the outlaw.

In the first paragraph the speaker imagines an Egyptian speaking to the Jewish refugees in his country, who would soon leave in search of the Promised Land, pursued by the army of Egypt. This orator then makes the point that the Ten Commandments ("the tables of the law") were engraved in stone by God in "the language of the outlaw," which is to say, in Hebrew. In its context, this is an argument for the Irish to recover their own language and escape the domination of English. For our purposes, however, it is a reminder that, if we are going to interpret a text like the Old Testament, we will need to read it in Hebrew ourselves, if we can, or consider various translations as approximations of the original. But if we assume that the God of the Hebrews is our God, we will have to treat this text as thoroughly sacred. Let us look, for a moment, at the relevant biblical passage in the English translation made in the time of Shakespeare—the King James Version:

1 And God spake all these words, saying,

2 I am the LORD thy God, which have brought thee out of the land of Egypt, out of the house of bondage.

3 Thou shalt have no other gods before me.

4 Thou shalt not make unto thee any graven image, or any likeness of any thing that is in heaven above, or that is in the earth beneath, or that is in the water under the earth:

5 Thou shalt not bow down thyself to them, nor serve them: for I the LORD thy God am a jealous God, visiting the iniquity of the fathers upon the children unto the third and fourth generation of them that hate me;

6 And shewing mercy unto thousands of them that love me, and keep my commandments. (Exodus 20:1–6)

This text appears to be as sacred as a text can get, since we are told in it that God is speaking directly, warning his audience that he is jealous and will punish his enemies for several generations. We had better understand him correctly and obey. But we are encountering God's words in English of a certain period, employing forms like "spake" and "shalt" that we no longer use. This reminds us that even the first Hebrew version of this text was written down at a particular time and place, and, as the scholars tell us, divided up into chapters and verses at another time. For this text to be perfectly sacred for us, we must accept this God as our God, and we must believe that the version we are reading has not lost, or gained, anything during its transmission and translation. It must be the same as the original. But the King James Version actually adapted the original to suit the audience of its own time. Arnold Hunt, in reviewing Naomi Tadmore's *The Social Universe of the English Bible* and other books on the King James Version (in the *Times Literary Supplement*, Feb. 11, 2011) put it this way:

Tadmore points to the virtual disappearance of slavery and polygamy from English Bibles. The word *eved* occurs 799 times in the Hebrew Bible, but its English counterpart, "slave," appears only once in the KJB's version of the Old Testament, which uses the word "servant" instead (or "handmaid" for female slaves) and reinterprets the language of bondage in terms of a legal contract or covenant.

Even with such changes, however, enough of the original frame of reference for this text comes through the Jacobean translation for us to recognize how different our world is from the world in which the Old Testament took shape. When, in a later commandment, we are told, "Thou shalt not covet thy neighbour's house, thou shalt not covet thy neighbour's wife, nor his manservant, nor his maidservant, nor his ox, nor his ass, nor any thing that is thy neighbour's" (20:17), we get a sense of how different our world is from the one in which these commandments were first recorded.

We are not likely to own or covet an ox or an ass, nor do we own servants, even if we are wealthy enough to hire them. A passage like this must be interpreted. If we assume that God was speaking to us as well as to Moses and his people, we must assume that he had to speak of the Hebrews' things in order for them to understand him. But, if he meant to refer to our world and our things as well, we must translate those ancient coveted objects into comparable features of our own world—oxen and asses into cars and trucks, for example—which is a basic act of interpretation. The notion of "sacredness" is something we apply to texts like this in order to constrain interpretation. To simply make sense of it in a basic way, however, we must perform an imaginative act, which tells us, I believe, that no text can be perfectly sacred in actuality—precisely because it is a text. Communication is never perfect, though simple things may be communicated between closely connected people with considerable accuracy. But even closely connected people often misunderstand one another. The popular cartoons that show a husband and wife and give us very different versions of "what she said" and "what he heard," or the reverse, direct our attention to this problem. When time, space, and language open wide the communicative gap, interpretation becomes more important—and more difficult.

In looking at this biblical passage, for example, we need to consider the audience. That is, we need to ask just who is being addressed and who is not. The wife, the servants, the ox, and the ass are not being addressed. They are understood to be possessions of the addressee. There is no edict against coveting a husband, because no one owns husbands. They are owners, possessors, not possessions; they are subjects, not objects. This God seems to be a male speaking to other males, in a world where women had few rights. Because this text is situated in a historical world, interpretation involves understanding how things were in that world. Extending interpretation to our own world without doing violence to that earlier one is no easy matter. If God does not change, but continues to be relevant, we must imagine that he appears in different ways to different peoples, speaking to them in their own languages and within their own cultural frames of reference—that he plays textual games. This raises the stakes of interpretation. The apostle Paul understood this perfectly, which is why (in 1 Corinthians) he speaks about being "made all things to all men" in order to save some of them. He is quite explicit about this:

20 And unto the Jews I became as a Jew, that I might gain the Jews; to them that are under the law, as under the law, that I might gain them that are under the law;

21 To them that are without law, as without law (being not without law to God, but under the law to Christ), that I might gain them that are without law.

22 To the weak became I as weak, that I might gain the weak:

I am made all things to all men, that I might by all means save some.

Here is a sacred text that reminds us in no uncertain terms of the necessity for interpretation, since we may be reading something originally composed by someone playing a role. If the central problem of interpretation is the search for meaning intended by the originator of the text, this search is made more difficult—and more interesting—when the originator admits to playing roles. But it is clear that we cannot simply react. We must interpret. With older texts there are other interpretive problems. We know very little about the origin of the really ancient religious texts, for example. There is evidence for multiple authorship of the first books of the Old Testament, but we have no direct information about who gathered those particular books and put them together in the first place, though we do know something about when and how certain books were included and others excluded from the finished sacred canon. The assumption that Moses wrote those first books gives interpretation a focus, but it is an assumption rejected by most biblical scholars.

With our sacred political texts in this country, however, we actually know a lot about how they were composed, what issues were debated before the final drafts were approved, and who wrote them down. This makes those documents ideal for the study of interpretation. Amendments to our Constitution, such as the ex- tension of the vote to different groups, offer excellent opportuni- ties for the study of arguments made on both sides of contested issues. The debate over women's suffrage is especially rich in this respect, and arguments against extending the vote to women often invoked biblical support. These debates went on for years, but finally the Constitution was amended and women received the vote in 1920. The Constitution avoided the word *slavery* but the problem remained and kept coming up as new states were added to the Union. Abraham Lincoln, in his "Cooper Union Address," gave us a brilliant example of an attempt to get at the hidden intentions of the Founding Fathers on this issue, by investigating their later votes on the question of the extension of slavery to the territories being elevated to statehood. But it took a bloody war to finally amend the document.

A Fundamental Problem

A few years ago, my wife and I were in the Prado, Madrid's great art museum, looking at some religious paintings, when a small boy and his parents came along. The child's mother explained to him what was going on in a painting of the crucifixion. This clearly upset him, and he began asking, "Why would anybody do that, why would anybody do that?" The parents did not come up with a simple and satisfactory answer. The one that ran through my own mind, however, was, "because the Romans did that to everybody," sometimes on a very large scale—as in the mass crucifixions, along the Appian Way, of six thousand slaves who had rebelled under the leadership of Spartacus. The biblical narratives tell us that two thieves were crucified along with Jesus, and some powerful paintings of the event show all three crucifixions. Still, over time, many Christians have tended to see this as an isolated episode in which one person suffered uniquely for the sins of all humankind. Yet this kind of brutality was relatively routine in the world of ancient Rome. This does not change the religious significance of the event for Christians, but it enables us to understand the cultural situation from which this Christian symbol emerged (and perhaps to ask ourselves how far we have progressed from that Roman culture). History also tells us that crucifixion was a specifically Roman punishment. Jews are often blamed for it, but the ancient Hebrews were more likely to have someone killed by throwing stones at them, as they did with the first Christian martyr, Saint Stephen. Cultural knowledge helps us see our texts more clearly.

The fact that the crucifixion was Roman is an important part of religious history. The church I grew up in is called the Roman Catholic Church for a reason. When Christianity took hold in Rome, the Roman Empire allowed it to spread far and wide. And when the empire fragmented into east and west, each part developed its own form of Christianity, with Roman Catholicism covering Western Europe and the Eastern Orthodox Church operating in the East. With the Reformation, other Christian sects split off from Catholicism into various kinds of Protestantism, generating their own versions of the sacred texts. And other religions, in many parts of the world, produced their own combinations of sacred history and rules for behavior. This process tends toward the production of a canon of sacred texts and leaves behind a body of excluded or apocryphal texts. What we have known as the literary canon was produced by a version of this religious process of inclusion and exclusion. In this book I am arguing against studying exclusively canonical literary works, but I am also advocating the study of works that have been given the most exclusive canonical status of sacredness.

One of the main functions of textual education is to help people learn how to see things from more than one perspective, and to understand that these perspectives are not exactly matters of choice for many people, but ways in which they have been conditioned to see the world. "To see ourselves as others see us" is important, but so is the ability to see others as they see themselves. One step toward this goal is to read sacred texts in this bi-focal manner. If we can learn to do it with these texts, we may learn to do it with all. But let us look, cautiously, at some of our own sacred texts and see what they have to teach us about reading. I want to frame this discussion with a quotation about the nature of interpretation, drawn from W. H. Auden's poem "The Orators." In these lines we hear a kind of commencement speech by a demented academic orator at a boys' school:

> What does it mean? What does it mean? Not what does it mean to them, there, then. What does it mean to us, here, now. It's a facer, isn't it, boys. But we've all got to answer it.

These words emphasize the fundamental problem of textual interpretation—that there is a gap, small or large, between the time and place of composition and the time and place of reception, and a gap in audiences, which means that there is likely to be a gap in understanding as well. Assumptions, presuppositions, values, experiences will not be exactly the same. Words change their meanings, sometimes minutely, sometimes drastically. Cultural values and expectations change. Auden's orator is ready to discard the original meanings in favor of contemporary ones. The fundamentalist position is ready to discard contemporary meanings and to insist on the original ones. The kind of reading I advocate calls for attention to both original and contemporary meanings. I do not intend to dismiss fundamentalism as a mode of reading, then, but rather to take it seriously, which is to say, critically.

Many people have thought that fundamentalist ways of thinking and reading would gradually lose their power as the world became progressively enlightened. Even Freud, who had many reasons to be skeptical about rationality, believed this. But it has *not* happened. Just ask those science teachers who are being directed to present creationism alongside evolution—if not instead of it—in some of our secondary schools. The appeals of fundamentalism are extremely powerful, and by no means confined to religion. Influential and extremely well-funded groups are attempting to read our Constitution and rewrite our laws in accordance with the letter of certain biblical texts—and to elect the legislators who will help them. There is a serious struggle here, worthy of our fullest attention and demanding of our greatest powers.

What does it mean to read a text in a *fundamentalist* way? Many people, including those who would take pride in being called fundamentalists, would describe fundamentalist reading as "literal" reading. So let us consider this word *literal* in a textualist way. The *lit* in literal refers to letters, a letter being the smallest legible part of a written word. But "literal" meaning is not the meaning of the letters, for meaning is not contained in individual letters but in such larger verbal units as prefixes, suffixes, and whole words. The concept of a literal meaning, then, is itself an exaggeration, a metaphor, a paradox. Nevertheless, it is an expression of a desire to get at the truth of a text, which we must respect and share, even as we insist on the complexity—if not the impossibility—of such a task.

The textualist reader, then, must acknowledge the seriousness of fundamentalist readings, while resisting and criticizing the zeal that often results in interpretive leaps to an unearned certainty of meaning, achieved by turning a deaf ear to the complexity of the texts themselves, their histories, and their present situations. As an example of fundamentalist reading, we can consider a statement made by the Southern Baptist Convention (SBC) in 1998, which affected the lives of thousands of people by insisting that wives must be subordinate to husbands—while also claiming that husband and wife were equals. This is not simply an issue for the SBC. The pope has said similar things. For our purposes what is important is the use of fundamentalist reading to regulate current human behavior. In this passage the SBC combines texts from the book of Genesis and the epistles of Paul to reach the following somewhat paradoxical conclusion:

> The husband and wife are of equal worth before God, since both are created in God's image. The marriage relationship models

the way God relates to his people. A husband is to love his wife as Christ loved the church. He has the God-given responsibility to provide for, to protect, and to lead his family. *A wife is to submit herself graciously to the servant leadership of her husband even as the church willingly submits to the headship of Christ.* She, being in the image of God as is her husband and thus equal to him, has the God-given responsibility to respect her husband and to serve as his helper in managing the household and nurturing the next generation. (emphasis added)

The part of this statement that I have italicized is an interpretation of the following lines from Paul: "Wives be subject to your husbands as to the Lord. For the husband is the head of the wife, as Christ also is the head of the Church, He Himself being the Savior of the body" (Ephesians 5:22–23). As an interpretation of Paul's words, the SBC seems to me to have got this just right. Paul, as is clear from many passages in his epistles, has in mind a hierarchy in which each level submits to the one above:

God
Christ
Church
Husband
Wife

But there are other things going on in the SBC's statement that are less straightforward. Twice in this short passage we are told that both husband and wife are equal because they are both "in the image of God." And we are also told that because they are equal the woman must be subordinate to the man. Such statements are not easy to read literally, for many reasons. One such reason is the difficulty of understanding just what is meant by "in the image." But this part of the SBC text does not come from Paul. It is based, rather, on the creation story from the book of Genesis.

As it happens, there are two versions of the creation in Genesis—one in 1:27 and another in 2:21–23. Scholars have told us that the two versions were produced by different people at different times, but that is not a path we can follow on this occasion. The first version is the one from which all attempts to ground the equality of the sexes in the creation narrative are drawn. It is very short, and it seems very clear. In this version it appears that both man and woman were created at the same time. Here is that version in a transcription of the original Hebrew, with a close translation:

v'yivrah HaElohim et HaAdam b'tsalmo, btselem Elohim bara oto, zachar oonikevah bara otam.
And God created the earthling, in His image, in the image of God, created He him, male and female, He created them.

In the second version God puts Adam to sleep after he has finished naming the animals, removes a rib from his side, and makes a creature out of it. But neither version says anything about this new creature being equal to man—and even the first version does not say that this creature is in the image of God. It says that the earthling or the Adam (*HaAdam* in the Hebrew) was created in the image of God, and that woman was created, too. It specifically does not say "in the image of God created he *her*." I find no license in this text for the assumption that the image of God is both male and female, or for the further assumption that a similarity of image would entail an equality of authority. Adam explains, when he names this new creation in the second version of the event, "she shall be called Woman because she is taken out of man" (2:23), reversing the biological birth process in doing so, and providing a rationale for male dominance that has persisted for centuries.

The reminders that man came first and has priority are constant in our language. Where, then, does the notion of "equality" come from? Not from Paul, certainly, for there are many passages in the

Pauline texts that insist on inequality and a difference, even, in the images of men and women, as in this crucial passage:

> But I want you to understand that Christ is the head of every man, and the man is the head of a woman, and God is the head of Christ. Every man who has something on his head while praying or prophesying, disgraces his head. But every woman who has her head uncovered while praying or prophesying, disgraces her head; for she is one and the same with she whose head is shaved. For if a woman does not cover her head, let her also have her hair cut off or her head shaved, let her cover her head. For a man ought not to have his head covered, since he is the image and glory of God; but the woman is the glory of man. For man does not originate from woman, but woman from man; for indeed man was not created for the woman's sake, but woman for the man's sake. *Therefore the woman ought to have a symbol of authority on her head, because of the angels.* However, in the Lord, neither is woman independent of man, nor is man independent of woman. (1 Corinthians 11:3–11; New American Standard Bible—in Kohlenberger—emphasis added)

Insofar as the Southern Baptist Convention's statement is a reading of this passage (which they cite in their literature), they are on strong ground with respect to the inequality of men and women. They would seem to be on weaker ground, however, in claiming equality on the basis of being created in the same image, for Paul makes it quite clear in the quoted passage that these are not equal images, with respect to hair at least. He also indicates that he reads the creation story as meaning that man is both the image and glory of God, but that woman is the glory of man—saying nothing about woman being in the image of either, and implying that she is different from both.

The hair passage is a little cryptic, but the general sense is clear.

Men should appear before God, in praying or prophesying, with no more covering on their heads than their hair. Women should not; a woman must have additional covering, "a symbol of authority on her head because of the angels," or, as the Greek original puts it, *dia tous aggelous*, which might also be translated "for the sake of the angels." If this passage made clear and simple sense to Paul and the Corinthians, it suggests a great cultural abyss between them and us, because it is very difficult for modern readers to imagine what those heavenly messengers had to do with hats. What does seem clear is that the covered head is a symbol of submission to authority, a sign of inequality, an inequality that is also presented through the metaphor of the body and the head, with man being the head of the female body. Any fundamentalist attempt to combine such texts as those of Genesis and Paul will lead to the paradox of some people being "more equal" than others, or a notion like the "servant leadership" of the husband over the wife.

We may attempt to generate fundamentalist readings of the Bible, based on the notion that the entire text is a divine utterance, with God speaking through all the voices that we hear in both the Old Testament and the New Testament. But even the simplest passages in these texts are not always easy to interpret. For example, in that short description of human creation in Genesis 1:27, the word for God presents problems. The Hebrew *HaElohim* is actually plural—meaning gods, not God—but the verb "created" (*v'yivrah*) is in the singular. Do we go with the noun or with the verb here? In practice most interpreters say that the plural is a kind of honorific term, like the "royal we" used by British rulers, as in Queen Victoria's famous, "We are not amused." But there are other interpreters who insist that the portion of Genesis in which the word *Elohim* is used was composed before monotheism became the settled belief, so that the word should indeed be read as a plural. Most Jewish and Christian interpreters, however, read this plural as a singular noun: "God" not "gods."

Any attempt to read these sacred texts inevitably encounters such conflicts or problems in interpretation, but fundamentalist reading normally rejects, denies, or conceals these difficulties, reducing meaning to what is already known or what is already allowed to be understood by the particular sect that claims authority over the text. Confronted by any particular anomaly resulting from an attempt to read a text literally, a reader trained in textuality will allow for an ambiguity or complexity that leaves the text open to further interpretation, while the fundamentalist reader will rely on accepted doctrine to force closure upon it. Interpretation of such texts is, and I want to emphasize this, a matter of getting it right, of reading gaps and contradictions in the text precisely as gaps and contradictions, rather than silently filling those gaps with ideological cement—which is what usually happens. But what is really required is scrupulous attention to what is left out of the text and what is self-contradictory in the text, as well as to what is said clearly in the text—whether we like what we are reading or not. In a textualist interpretation, we give "them, there, then" their due.

We must seek an original intention, then, while recognizing that there are many reasons why we shall never close the gap that separates us from the original author or authors, for the sacred texts cannot always be read directly. The apostle Paul was well aware of this. He himself recommends reading not literally, according to "the letter," but according to "the spirit"—"for the letter (*gramma*) kills, but the spirit (*pneuma*) gives life" (2 Corinthians 3:6). Looking at these few passages from biblical texts has demonstrated, I trust, that the interpretation of sacred texts is important—and difficult. These are texts that affect our lives in powerful ways. Are women really equal to men—or not? There are cultures today that have all sorts of rules for the garments women must wear. And others that are making laws forbidding the public imposition of these religious rules. One thing we should learn, then, from looking at the Pauline rules for women's clothing, is that Paul lived in a culture that was closer to those that presently have such rules than to our own, which means that reading him in a truly fundamentalist way will take us closer to those cultures. So, we must decide, in the critical phase of reading these texts, whether we wish to make that move, or decide that portions of what Paul says must be rejected because they fit his culture but not ours. And there is more than clothing at stake in this decision, since Paul also addresses the question of women speaking in church or teaching. In the First Epistle to Timothy (chapter 2) Paul writes:

11 Let a woman quietly receive instruction with entire submissiveness.
12 But I do not allow a woman to teach or exercise authority over a man, but to remain quiet.

And in 1 Corinthians (chapter 14):

34 Let the women keep silent in the churches; for they are not permitted to speak, but let them subject themselves, just as the Law also says.
35 And if they desire to learn anything, let them ask their own husbands at home; for it is improper for a woman to speak in church.

It is clear, I believe, where Paul stands in these matters. He was a man of his time, which is not our time, which means that we should read his work critically. Actually, women in the United States have been reading these sacred texts critically for some time. In 1895, for example, Elizabeth Cady Stanton published *The Woman's Bible*, noting in her introduction that "[f]rom the inauguration of the movement for woman's emancipation the Bible has been used to hold her in the 'divinely ordained sphere,' prescribed in the Old and New Testaments" (7). A century later (in 1992) Carol

A. Newsom and Sharon H. Ringe produced *The Women's Bible Commentary*, which begins with this paragraph:

> What on earth does the Bible mean? How can modern readers ever understand the assumptions and language taken for granted by ancient authors and their communities? When the reader is a woman, how is the *process* of reading the Bible, or the *result* of that process, different? How has the Bible influenced the lives of women and men through history and in the present? How ought it to shape the lives of women and men who look to it as the norm for faith and practice? What does it mean to call the Bible "the word of God"? What might compel one to say, "On this point the Bible is wrong"? At the heart of such questions is the process of interpretation.

To which I can only respond with "Amen, sisters." A textualist reading of Paul, in particular, has been implicit in my discussion of the fundamentalist readings, but perhaps, before concluding, I should pull those implications together and make my notion of such a reading more explicit. To read Paul's epistles in a textualist way means attempting to situate the text and the writer of these letters in their own time, constructing, from the clues in the text, the persona of this writer, paying particular attention to his self-fashioning. As he tells his correspondents about his own sufferings for the cause, his imprisonment and beatings; as he returns again and again to the issue of sexual purity, stressing his own celibate status as a human ideal; as he addresses simple, personal remarks to this or that individual—he constructs a persona, a character, who is a version of the author of the text. A textualist reading would interrogate the reliability of that figure, and factor it into the reception of what he says. Such a reading would also take note of the gaps and the contradictions in the text. The reader should recognize and even admire Paul's rhetorical power as a writer, and should follow his subtle shifts as a reader, as when he moves from literal to allegorical or spiritual modes of interpretation of earlier texts. The goal of this kind of reading would be to comprehend, as well as possible, Paul's presuppositions, to understand as fully as possible his prescriptions for human conduct, and, finally, having established to the best of our ability what this text meant to "them, there, then," to ask what it should mean to "us, here, now." That is, we must try to determine the text's proper bearing on our own values and our conduct in the world.

To read the biblical text in this way would be to recognize its complexity and to move from interpretation to criticism, thus giving readers the freedom to accept or reject the values they have discovered there. And this is just what fundamentalism cannot allow. For true believers, whether Christian or Muslim, Stalinist or Maoist, the tables of the law are written in stone, not in the human heart. They know the letter of the law already, and so need not read in a textualist way. That is why they cherish the letter and mistrust the spirit of the text. Above all, they cannot accept this basic premise of modern textual interpretation: that never in this life will we see the text face to face, but always as through a glass, darkly, so that we can only read and reread, to the best of our ability, unless we choose to cover our heads and bow to authority, "because of the angels."

A Failure to Communicate

For some years our country has been involved, in one way or another, with political problems in the Muslim world, and we have often tried to deal with them in military ways, without much success. Most of us do not know the sacred texts of Islam well enough to use them effectively in our classrooms, though perhaps that will change in the future. Nevertheless, we may find in Christian texts some useful ideas about that part of the world, if we will pay attention to them, for this is clearly a world of sacred texts and holy places. Let us enter it, then, on the road to Damascus, a city which lies between Jerusalem and Teheran. A great master of textual rhetoric has been on this road before us, and I propose that we follow him. The person we are following is called "Saul" in the Acts of the Apostles, and he turns up on the road to Damascus in Acts 9:3. This is not, however, the first time he has appeared in this text. He came on stage in an earlier scene in an intriguing role. The false witnesses, who had been suborned to testify at the trial of Stephen, appeared at his subsequent execution, and "laid down their garments at the feet of a young man named Saul" (Acts 7:58). It is by no means clear why Saul got their garments, but it looks as if he had been in charge of some aspects of the rigged trial and stoning to death of the first Christian martyr. When Stephen asks God not to blame those who have stoned him and then falls "asleep," as the Greek text puts it, we are told unequivocally that "Saul was consenting unto his death" (Acts 8:1), or, in the New Revised Standard Version, "Saul approved of their killing him."

Nor did Saul's dirty work stop there. After Stephen's burial, Saul got busy: "Saul laid waste the church, entering into every house, and dragging men and women committed them to prison" (Acts 8:3). Saul's actions have an eerie familiarity to present-day events. He was working for the Jewish high priests, we must remember, persecuting the Christians on their behalf. The Acts of the Apostles are notable for the way in which they position the Jews as the oppressors of the early disciples of Christ. (This is a source that has fueled anti-Semitism for centuries.) But we must continue to follow Saul for a while. In Acts 9:1 and 9:2 we find him busy again at his persecution: "Saul, yet breathing threatening and slaughter against the disciples of the Lord, went unto the high priest, and asked of him letters to Damascus unto the synagogues, that if he found any that were of the Way, whether men or women, he might bring them bound to Jerusalem."

Saul did not have a Guantanamo, but he did the best he could, and he was on his way to Damascus to round up the usual suspects when the part of this story that is familiar to most of us took place. The Lord appeared to him, knocked him down and left him temporarily blinded. Three days later "the scales fell from his eyes," he saw the light, and became a follower of the Christian Way. This Saul of Tarsus was a man of action, however, and he was not going to hide his new light under a bushel. But what he did and did not do next is very interesting. He did not take up arms for his new faith; rather he went to the synagogues of Damascus and preached there:

> 9:20 And straightway in the synagogues he proclaimed Jesus, that he is the Son of God.
>
> 9:21 And all that heard him were amazed, and said, Is not this he that in Jerusalem made havoc of them that called on this name? and he had come hither for this intent, that he might bring them bound before the chief priests.

In short, he took the risk of professing his new faith but he did not fight for it. This may have been mere prudence, the actions of a member of a minority sect too weak to challenge its enemy by force, but I prefer to think of it as an aspect of his change of heart, his conversion to a new faith that believed in the word as being more powerful than the sword. As a Christian he suffers violence but never uses or advocates it. But we are pulling a single narrative thread out of a complex text, here, and interpreting the meaning of that thread.

And the thread goes on. Saul, having been endangered by his preaching, learned that "the Jews took counsel together to kill him" (Acts 9:23), so he was smuggled out of Damascus by being lowered over the wall in a basket, thus avoiding the guarded gates. On his return to Jerusalem, we are told, Saul met with the apostles and preached with them, but the city was too dangerous for him and he was told to go home to Tarsus and hide there. Later, Peter brought him out of Tarsus and set Saul on his apostolic career. They preached together in Antioch and it was there that the followers of Jesus were first called Christians. Shortly after this we learn for the first time that Saul was also called "Paul," and the rest, as they say, is history—or rhetoric. Anyway, it is scripture. And Paul became the most eloquent and powerful shaper of Christian doctrine after Jesus himself. The narrative thread involving Paul goes on, but our interest in him changes from interest in a character whose deeds are narrated in the third person to interest in an author who speaks in the first person and addresses his audience directly in his famous epistles.

There is another grammatical shift, however, that occurs within the Acts of the Apostles that we should note before moving on. Shortly after Peter and Paul join forces, the narrative voice of the book of Acts makes a drastic change. Here is the passage in which it happens:

> 16:8 And when they were come over against Mysia, *they* assayed to go into Bithynia; and the Spirit of Jesus suffered them not; and passing by Mysia, they came down to Troas.
> 16:9 And a vision appeared to Paul in the night: There was a man of Macedonia standing, beseeching him, and saying, Come over into Macedonia, and help us.
> 16:10 And when *he* had seen the vision, straightway *we* sought to go forth into Macedonia, concluding that God had called *us* to preach the gospel to them. (emphasis added)

The shift here is from third person (they, he) to describe the deeds of these apostles to the first person (we, us). For students of narrative rhetoric this is a truly remarkable event. The narrator, who had been positioned outside the story, recording it for others, suddenly moves inside it. But this narrator still refers to Paul as "he," locating himself as a companion. This companion is usually identified as Luke by biblical scholars, making him the author of this text as well as one of the first three gospels.

The Acts are a text, we should note, in which the spread of Christianity is presented as heavily dependent upon miracles: the dead brought back to life, the crippled cured and enabled to walk, and so on. But it is always about spreading the word, which is to say, it is rhetorical to the core. When Saul converted from Judaism to the Way that came to be called Christianity, he also converted from being a thug working for the high priests to being one of a group of equals who relied on words to do their work and risked martyrdom for their cause. This change is enacted in Luke's grammatical move from "they" to "we," which signifies an acceptance of equality and cooperation, and a bearing of witness, a giving up of the anonymous position sometimes called "omniscient" for a position within the text as an identifiable human being. Within this narrative, however, Paul is still an object and not yet a subject of the discourse, though he is singled out by Luke as of special importance. At one point certain men come "following after Paul and us," but when Paul and Silas are captured by a mob and beaten, it is "they" not "we" who suffer. Where, we may well wonder, was that cool hand, Luke, when this happened?

One of the things we can learn from this passage is that grammar is important—it is in fact a crucial aspect of narrative structure—especially when it comes to something as consequential as the rise of Christianity. Other things are also important. In the Acts of the Apostles, conversions are represented as heavily dependent upon miracles. But there was clearly another factor. Paul's own epistles, in which we hear the voice of a master of rhetoric, depend more upon this rhetoric than on miraculous interventions.

I often wonder why we Americans, claiming to be a Christian nation, do not emulate Paul more closely. That is, I wonder why we do not have more confidence in our message and rely less on thuggery and violence. How can we proclaim to the world our right to torture and martyr other people, while still maintaining that we are a nation of virtue? If we think we can save our souls for eternity, why are we so worried about an act of earthly terrorism against us? Why do we insist on behaving like Saul the secret operative instead of like Paul the rhetorician? Why don't we have more faith in the power of the word and make a real effort to win the propaganda battle which we are presently losing all over the world? As you will have noted, these questions look and sound like what we call "rhetorical" questions, but they are also real questions—questions to which I do not know the answers. I know that we are doing something wrong as a nation, wrong both in principle and in practice. But I wonder if we—as a people—or the leaders who speak for us—believe in the principles we and they profess—whether those principles be Christian or democratic. I am not a Christian myself, though I have been one; I am an atheist. And my concerns here are not religious—or political—but rhetorical. It seems to me, however, that we are doing a bad job of interpreting the motives of those whom we believe threaten us and a worse job of winning others to our side in these troubled times.

It was Paul, as we have seen, who said "I have fought a good fight. I have finished the course. I have kept the faith." As we know, however, he had been on a different course until he flip-flopped on the way to Damascus. This change, from force to rhetoric as a method of converting people to his way of thinking, was a change from the old beliefs, the Law, to new ones—the Way. I want to argue that—as a country—we need to learn two lessons from this text. One is that a reversal of course can be the right thing to do. And the other is that rhetoric is more effective than force as a method of persuasion. What we have here is "a failure to communicate." Knowing what happened to the character (whose name, as it happens, was Luke) who repeated those words in a movie—right after he said them,—I will stop at this point.

Lots of Folks Forget That Part of It

Sacred texts come in more than one form and from more than one source, but the two main sources are those sanctioned by a religion and those sanctioned by a government. In the United States there is no text more sacred than our Declaration of Independence, which was composed, of course, before we were the United States. It was used, you will remember, in *The Man Who Shot Liberty Valance*, by Ransom Stoddard to teach reading to his class of illiterates in Shinbone. I wish to use it in another way here—actually, in more ways than one. The first way is as part of my argument that we should be teaching the sacred texts of our culture precisely because they are sacred. They affect us all. They are powerful. And we tend to take them for granted, without actually reading them—which brings me to the other ways in which I mean to use this text. We hear a lot, these days, about judicial interpretation, about how judges are supposed to read and interpret the words of our sacred governmental texts. Should the construction of meaning be "strict" or "loose," for example. If we look closely enough, we will find that the problems of fundamentalist reading also arise in cases of "strict" judicial construction, which is a mode of secular fundamentalism. Obviously, "loose" construction can't be good. It is just a euphemistic way of pointing to sloppy reading. But absolutely "strict" construction is strictly impossible—or it wouldn't be construction at all.

Construction, in this sense, is a form of interpretation, and interpretation involves bringing the knowledge of the interpreter to bear on the text that is being read. It involves adding something to the text. The advocates of strictness will argue that what is added must be in the service of divining the intentions of the creator of the text and making them explicit when applying them to new situations. I am sympathetic to this notion of respecting the intentions of the authors of texts. I believe it is a fundamental part of the interpretive process. But it is not the only part, or the last step. It can't be the whole of any process of reading. Furthermore, the greater the gap between the origin of a text and its interpretation, the more difficult and complex that interpretation becomes. The writers of a political text, or a legal text, cannot foresee all the instances in which their words may be invoked, or what changes may occur in the course of human events, making their words less applicable to the situations to which they may be applied. And our most sacred political text assures us that there is indeed a "Course of human events" which brings about changes in political and legal situations. Before turning to that sacred political text, I want to consider another very short one, which has been a frequent focus of debates about strict interpretation. This text is the Second Amendment to the U. S. Constitution:

> A well regulated militia, being necessary to the security of a free state, the right of the people to keep and bear arms, shall not be infringed.

Supposedly strict construction has functioned to read this text as allowing everybody to own as many weapons as they want and even to carry them wherever they wish to, because "the right of the people to keep and bear arms shall not be infringed." But a really strict interpretation of this law would have to ask what kind of arms the authors could have had in mind, as well as what they meant by a "well regulated militia." Could they have been thinking of weapons that had not yet been invented when they wrote these words and voted on them? Could they have meant to include automatic rifles, machine guns, grenades, and weapons of mass destruction? Did they mean, for instance, to protect a person's right to walk around in an explosive vest in a crowded place? Questions of history and technology are involved in the notion of "arms." If we stick to the arms known by the authors of this amendment in 1791, interpreting as strictly as possible, we get one kind of law. If we allow all kinds of weapons invented since, we get another. If we stop the interpretive process at various points in the chain of development, we will get as many interpretations as there are stopping points. Do we stop with the revolver? the Kalashnikov? with suicide bombs? with biological weapons?

These problems come up even before we decide what a "well regulated militia" meant in 1791 and what it might mean now. It could mean that now only members of the National Guard should have the right to bear arms, if we think of the National Guard as a well-regulated militia. But that part of the text is usually ignored by those who take positions advocated by the National Rifle Association. They don't like "regulation" in any form, or rather they will allow the regulation of militias but not the regulation of guns. I do not wish to argue with any particular position here, only to show that the interpretation of this sacred political text is not easy to settle by applying the oxymoronic notion of strict construction. But now let us turn to an even more fundamental text in our political world:

> When in the Course of human events, it becomes necessary for one people to dissolve the political bands which have connected them with another, and to assume among the powers of the earth, the separate and equal station to which the Laws of Nature and of Nature's God entitle them, a decent respect to the opinions of mankind requires that they should declare the causes which impel them to the separation.

Because this is a historical document, rather than a text from a relatively undocumented era, we have a fair amount of information about when and where was it written, how was it disseminated, who wrote it, and so on, but before using that information, let us just examine those words, seeing what sense we can make of them.

We can begin with the first word: *When*. This is a word of temporality. It situates us in a particular moment. The whole phrase, "When in the Course of human events," tells us that the moment is a historical one. This phrase assumes that human events are neither random nor static. They are composed in a "Course." They have a direction, which we have learned to call history. The paragraph consists of a single complex sentence, followed by a long dash separating it from the next paragraph. The next section of this first sentence informs us that within this historical moment, this "When," it has become "necessary" for "one people" to "dissolve" certain "political bands" which connect them to another people. Before we explore the meanings of these words we must back up to the top of the document. The first line of text says, "IN CONGRESS, July 4, 1776." And the second adds, "The unanimous Declaration of the thirteen united States of America," ending in a comma, pointing across a considerable gap to the word *When*. This date helps us with the "When," and the second line helps us with the expression "one people." These people are the inhabitants of the "thirteen united States of America." Notice that the word *united* is not capitalized. The "United States of America" was not yet a name. There were thirteen "States" and they were united. We are also told that they were "unanimous" in making the declaration that appeared below this line. Can that word be interpreted literally or "strictly"? Certainly not, if it applies to all the citizens of those thirteen colonies now calling themselves "States." There were many who opposed the American Revolution, including some who left for Canada or the Bahamas and others who stayed, unhappily, through the years of war that followed.

But the fifty-six people who signed this document were indeed unanimous, and they represented "IN CONGRESS" the citizens of those states. This unanimity, however, had been hammered out in contentious meetings, by people who were told that if they did not "hang together" they might be hanged separately. There are a lot of excellent digital resources on this document, and students should be encouraged to make the most of them. The challenge, however, is to see freshly a text that has almost been venerated to death. And to see it as a textual problem, requiring interpretation, rather than as a piece of history to be accepted and forgotten. Above all, in this opening sentence, we need to see what is being avoided or suppressed. The word *nation*, for example, does not appear. We have "people" and "powers" instead of the political entities called nations. Not yet being a nation, though aspiring to be one, these thirteen states present themselves as a "people" who wish to join the "powers" of the earth as a separate and equal member of that group. The problem of acting like a nation without being one is cleverly solved by the terminology adopted here.

The "station" which these people wish to assume is defined as one to which they are entitled by "the Laws of Nature and of Nature's God." A world view is encapsulated in this phrase—a view of the natural world as governed by laws (like the law of gravity), which imply a lawmaker who has constructed this orderly world—a world in which everything has a place. If we are going to read sacred texts—or any texts—well, we cannot stop with interpretation. We must go on to criticism. And in this case, we must ask how the laws of nature entitle any "people" to an equal place among the "powers of the earth." Looking toward the future from 1776 to 1861, we might ask whether the eleven states of the Confederacy were not a people entitled to become a separate power by the same Laws of Nature invoked by the thirteen states in the previous century. In actuality, both issues were decided on the battlefields. A "people" become a "power" by winning a struggle—and fail by losing one. Not all struggles involve warfare. Passive resistance has worked in some cases. But the Laws of Nature do not settle issues of this kind. Their invocation in this document is one of the elements that situates the "When" from which it emerges. It is a document of the Enlightenment, based on a view of the world as an orderly place constructed by a rational God—a view that is apparent throughout this text. We must ask, in any reading of this document, whether that worldview should still be seen as operative in our own quite different world, just as we must ask about the changes in meaning of particular words since they were first written.

Another aspect of reading any text that comes to us from another time or place involves placing the audience. Who is being addressed in this text, and how is our situation like and unlike theirs? Most biblical texts, for example, were addressed to people whose situations were very different from our own. But even our sacred political texts were not addressed directly to people quite like us, a fact which becomes more and more apparent as we push on through the opening paragraphs. As with many other such texts, this one has more than one audience in mind. The audience that is named in the opening sentence is "mankind," whose opinions are to be respected. The document is meant to persuade this audience of the justice of the colonial cause and the rationality of its government. But "mankind" is an impossibly vague concept. In fact, two distinct but specific audiences are being addressed here: the British "people" and the American. We know that the French were being wooed as well, but not by merely verbal means. The "united States" were offering them an opportunity to damage their enemy, Great Britain, and their ultimate acceptance of that offer had more to do with the happy result of the affair than either the Laws of Nature or the rhetoric of Jefferson and his associates.

The document goes on to blame King George III for having brought things to this pass. It is ostensibly addressed to him, but it was really aimed at the British people and their Parliament, in an attempt to separate them from their incompetent if not insane ruler. It is also aimed closer to home. The original was on parchment, but around two hundred printed copies were circulated as broadsides and read aloud in public squares and to the troops as well. The printed version has a slightly different heading from the manuscript:

In CONGRESS, July 4, 1776.
A DECLARATION
By the REPRESENTATIVES of the
UNITED STATES OF AMERICA,
In GENERAL CONGRESS assembled.

The word *unanimous* has been dropped, and the number "thirteen" has disappeared as well. In place of "unanimous" we now have the "REPRESENTATIVES" of the unnumbered "UNITED STATES OF AMERICA." We know that the printer worked with Franklin and Jefferson close at hand, and we can see that these changes are clearly improvements in the document, making it look more like something produced by the government of a country and less like the work of a committee making extravagant claims on behalf of thirteen colonies. But this is clearly a case where the interpreter must choose between texts in deciding which is the more authentic expression of the authors' final intentions.

The idea of having a decent respect for the opinions of mankind suggests the possibility of a world order, an international system of values if not of laws. Having opened this door toward the future, the document proceeds to suggest that all mankind should accept certain views as self-evident truths, making its point in such a way that it has become the most famous bit of language in the entire document: "We hold these truths to be self-evident, that all men are created equal, that they are endowed by their Creator with certain unalienable Rights, that among these are Life, Liberty and the pursuit of Happiness." Here, again, the notion of a rational God appears, in this case conferring rights upon all the men he has created. They have the rights that this God has bestowed upon them, and they require, as the document goes on to argue, that governments be organized in order to maintain these rights, and thus must always function with the consent of those governed. When Abraham Lincoln was assassinated, his killer shouted "*Sic semper tyrannis*" (thus always to tyrants), which happened to be the state motto of Virginia. The phrase is attributed to Brutus, one of the killers of Julius Caesar, with Brutus justifying this assassination as an attempt to preserve the Roman Republic against what he saw as a despotic usurpation. The cry of the assassin of Lincoln can also be read as an attempt to invoke the Declaration of Independence, on the grounds that Lincoln's government had just imposed its will on the rebellious states without the consent of the people of those states, including Virginia, which had played such a large part in the original Declaration, through the textual efforts of Thomas Jefferson.

But there are other points of interest in this sentence for the reader of sacred texts. As we have noted, it comes up in the classroom where Ransom Stoddard is teaching illiterates in *The Man Who Shot Liberty Valance*. The texts for the day on which we observe this classroom are the current issue of the *Shinbone Star* and the Declaration of Independence. The older students have been studying the Constitution and the Declaration as part of their basic reading instruction, while the young ones have been learning their ABCs. When the only black person in the class, Tom Doniphan's servant Pompey, tries in vain to remember the sentence about all men being created equal, Ransom gently finishes it for him and observes that "[l]ots of folks forget that part of it." Pompey is also confused about the source, thinking this is from the Constitution, and Stoddard quietly corrects him about this in the film as well (though not in the novelization of the film by J. W. Bellah). We are still working on that one, it appears. But what does the statement mean, anyway? How should we read it? Do we begin by asking what the fifty-six white males who signed the document could have meant by it? Or do we ask what it means to us, here and now? A strict constructionist would insist that we must consider the intentions of the signers and only those. But can we assume that fifty-six people had a single intention?

In the present case, we can assume that "all men" does not include women, since they had no representatives in this group. And we know that it does not include African-American slaves, because slaves are not entitled to liberty, as the other sacred texts endorsed by the Founding Fathers make perfectly clear. Article IV of the Constitution, for example, says that "[n]o person held to service or labor in one state, under the laws thereof, escaping into another, shall, in consequence of any law or regulation therein, be discharged from such service or labor, but shall be delivered up on claim of the party to whom such service or labor may be due"—which meant that escaped slaves had to be returned to their owners, even if they escaped to a state that had forbidden slavery, though the language is strangely euphemistic, suggesting some embarrassment on the part of the authors. We also know that during debates about how a census of the population should be taken to determine the number of congressional representatives allotted to each state, it was agreed that each slave would be counted as three fifths of a person. It was only in 1870, after the Civil War, that the Fifteenth Amendment to the Constitution was passed, stating that "[t]he right of citizens of the United States to vote shall not be denied or abridged by the United States or by any state on account of race, color, or previous condition of servitude."

We should note two things about this amendment. It tells us that former slaves could vote (that "previous condition of servitude") and it does not mention sex or gender. The voting rights of women of any race were not protected until another half century had passed, which makes it quite clear that women were a forgotten part of all the "men" who were held to have been created equal in that original sacred text. These amendments, and a number of others, came about because a reading of the original documents, with close attention to the assumed intentions of the composers of those documents, indicated that they were needed—because those intentions were subject to a critical reading that found them wanting in the light of social changes. The sacred texts of government can be changed, though the process is not easy. The sacred texts of religions, however, are yet another story. Consider, for example, some famous lines from Deuteronomy, chapter 7, in which the Israelites are advised how to treat various powerful groups around them:

2 And when the LORD thy God shall deliver them before thee; thou shalt smite them, and utterly destroy them; thou shalt make no covenant with them, nor show mercy unto them:

3 Neither shalt thou make marriages with them; thy daughter thou shalt not give unto his son, nor his daughter shalt thou take unto thy son.

4 For they will turn away thy son from following me, that they may serve other gods: so will the anger of the LORD be kindled against you, and destroy thee suddenly.

5 But thus shall ye deal with them; ye shall destroy their altars, and break down their images, and cut down their groves, and burn their graven images with fire.

6 For thou art an holy people unto the LORD thy God: the LORD thy God hath chosen thee to be a special people unto himself, above all people that are upon the face of the earth.

Whose words are these? And should they mean to "us, here, now," what they meant to "them, there, then"? Or should we say that times have changed and these words no longer apply to our world—at the risk of allowing the author to appear less divine? There are people in Israel today who take this text as a promise that they are indeed chosen to rule over everyone in their area. And there are others in that land who say they are historically important but no longer to be read as a guide for present life. There is a comparable passage in chapter 2 of the Quran, which goes this way in the Shakir translation:

190 And fight in the way of Allah with those who fight with you, and do not exceed the limits, surely Allah does not love those who exceed the limits.

191 And kill them wherever you find them, and drive them out from whence they drove you out, and persecution is severer than slaughter, and do not fight with them at the Sacred Mosque until they fight with you in it, but if they do fight you, then slay them; such is the recompense of the unbelievers.

192 But if they desist, then surely Allah is Forgiving, Merciful.

193 And fight with them until there is no persecution, and religion should be only for Allah, but if they desist, then there should be no hostility except against the oppressors.

This injunction to fight for a particular faith is somewhat gentler than the one in Deuteronomy, more concerned with defense and readier to forgive the enemy. There are other passages in the full text, however, that are less conciliatory, but I do not wish to rank or judge these two sacred texts. I quote them both simply to show that these texts offer instructions from earlier times, which can be accepted without criticism or modified to suit present circumstances. In our present world, this sort of interpretive and critical choice may indeed be a matter of life or death. Ordinary human possibilities and opportunities may also depend on how we read these ancient texts. If the sacred religious text says that women must keep their hair covered "because of the angels" then either they must do that—always and everywhere the angels may lurk—or the text must be criticized to limit its application. One might say, for instance, that the author spoke only for himself and not for God in this instance.

If the text says women must not teach, the same principles apply. Does "teach" mean all teaching or only religious teaching—or specifically teaching inside a church? What sorts of teaching may women be allowed to do? Are there some sorts that should be forbidden? There are, of course, Christian sects in which women can serve as priests and others in which they cannot. But even Roman Catholic nuns are allowed to teach. I was taught by them in "Sunday School" (on Wednesday afternoons). In the larger world, if the text says that we must destroy those who believe in other faiths, should we attempt to do that and institute religious wars? There are people who think that some sort of crusade or jihad is the right thing for them to undertake—and they belong to more than one faith. And there are other people who think we should indeed make covenants with those of other beliefs and end hostilities. The sacred texts of religion lead us to these critical decisions if we interpret them carefully, just as the sacred texts of politics lead to questions about constitutional amendments and changes to the law. There is no end to discussion of these crucial texts, but this chapter must end now, because it is time to consider the reading of profane texts, which must also be part of the study and teaching of textuality.

CHAPTER FIVE

Textual Pleasure—Profane Reading

ALL TEXTS THAT ARE NOT ACCORDED SACRED STATUS MAY BE considered profane—especially if we can do away with the semi-sacred category of literature. I have already offered some demonstrations of ways to deal with a range of texts inside and outside the current boundaries of literature, and I have argued that we need to read texts accorded sacred status with special attention to the claims about truth and law that they make. But the world of textuality is not divided equally into sacred and profane sets of texts. The shape of this world is more like a sphere, with a relatively small set of sacred texts at the center and large groups of others at varying distances and directions from that center, which means that students of textuality should encounter sacred texts and some set or sets of the others. In another book (*Modernism in the Magazines: An Introduction*), I have discussed one set of profane texts—periodicals of the early twentieth century—trying to suggest how they should be read and how all their contents, from poetry to advertising, should be considered. I will not repeat that here, but move to another set of texts that are a long way from attaining sacred status—texts that acknowledge their distance from truth and reality, emphasizing, instead, their desire to please audiences. Because of their distance from the sacred center, my main concern will be to make the case for their inclusion in the textual curriculum, rather than to demonstrate how they should be interpreted and criticized, though I shall offer some suggestions about this. When Dr. Johnson praised Goldsmith for writing a play that made the audience merry, he was talking about a central feature of this set of texts. Many of them present us with painful events, but in such a way as to remind us that we are not looking at life itself but at an artificial representation of it, which removes the sting, to some extent.

The texts I have chosen to discuss in this chapter all tell stories, and they all go beyond the world of words, adding images and music in presenting the stories they tell. Moreover, they all enact or perform those stories, connecting the world of print to that of the stage or screen. Representations of musical drama, including opera, will play a central role in this chapter, because they are situated at an extreme distance from the sacred and the purely verbal. The pedagogical uses of opera were brought home to me a few years ago, when I was working with a group of high school teachers, designing a course called "Pacesetter English," in which one unit was to be based on a play by Shakespeare. We had chosen *Othello*, and were looking at videos of all the performances we could find, to see which actor had embodied the title character most adequately. We looked at American, British, and South African performers, without being fully satisfied with any we saw. Finally, almost for recreation, I showed a video I had brought to the conference, of Placido Domingo playing the leading role in Verdi's opera *Otello*. Unanimously, the group said, in effect, "that's the one, that's the best Othello." And we began to discuss how the opera might be used in the course.

There are interesting differences between the opera's libretto by Arrigo Boito and Shakespeare's play, including a soliloquy given to Iago in the opera that helps explain his motivation, but there is music in the play, as well, with Desdemona singing the "Willow Song" just before her death. Looking at the opera along with the play opens up many directions for discussion and writing. Powerful texts cross media all the time, remaining the same while becoming different. But operas are a neglected resource in teaching, partly because so many are in languages other than English, and partly because they belong to yet another department in our divided academic world. Even so, there are great operas in English, and one of the greatest is a text in which jazz and classical music mingle in a world that is as profane as possible, with a source in a popular novel, and performances that have ranged from Broadway to the Metropolitan Opera and other great opera houses around the world.

Many of the world's great works of fiction and drama have operatic incarnations. But I also want to direct attention to more humble works that combine words, images, music, and performance. I believe that operas and other music dramas should get more attention in our curricula, because there is much to be learned from them, and especially from their artificiality—their rejection of sacred status. They will tell us lies and challenge us to find the truth in them, if we can, which means that our readings of such texts must begin by noting the ways in which they proclaim their fictional relationship to reality, and then continue by considering what these lies may be telling us about the truth. These texts also offer a special educational opportunity because they exist in different forms. Many of them began their lives in a different medium. There are operatic versions, for example, of *Hamlet*, *Macbeth*, *Romeo and Juliet*, *Othello*, *Much Ado About Nothing*, and other Shakespeare plays, and musical settings of scenes or moments from his plays, like Hector Berlioz's version of Cleopatra's death. All these can be used to provide another angle of approach to Shakespeare. There are also other music dramas derived from novels, plays, stories—and even from films, as we shall see—and such dramas can be studied profitably with their sources. This kind of study, which we may call "comparative textuality," makes it easier for students to consider questions of interpretation and critical judgment, because, instead of facing a single, apparently inviolable text, they have different versions to compare.

For most operas, recordings come with librettos in the original language, accompanied by translations into several others, including English. Treating an opera as a text means using the libretto, listening to recordings, looking at videos, and helping students learn to use such resources themselves. Since each performance is an interpretation of the words and the musical score, with its own staging and costumes, its own choices about how each role should be played, studying performances of an opera opens the way to interpretation by the reader / viewer. Moreover, if the opera or music drama is based on a text in another medium, it is itself an interpretation or revision of that earlier text. We have seen how *The Man Who Shot Liberty Valance* moved from story to film to novel, offering opportunities for teaching by a comparison of the different versions. Most music dramas provide comparable opportunities. And their multilingual librettos direct attention to language in a special way. In a music department, of course, one would also look at the score of a work and consider that as a basic text, but it is not necessary to go that far in order to use music drama in a course in textuality. Looking at the original language of an important moment in an opera, however, can help increase a student's awareness of language in general.

Different performances of music dramas—and even performances of particular songs or arias—open the way to criticism. Comparing one performance with another allows us not only to evaluate them against one another but also encourages us to consider the question of which interpretation captures the original most successfully—and which is the most suitable for audiences today. Because performative works depend on audiences, the question of what they mean to "us, here, now" gains in importance. We live in a performative world, which is another reason why we should pay special attention to enacted stories in our classrooms. Shakespeare's slightly clownish academic, Jacques, suggested long ago that life is a kind of theatrical performance:

All the world's a stage,
And all the men and women merely players;
They have their exits and their entrances;
And one man in his time plays many parts. . . .

We can learn a lot by considering the ways in which this both is and
is not true. Most of the texts I have chosen here explore the nature
of performance itself, and the extent to which life itself offers roles,
turning people into clowns or lovers—or some combination of
the two. But they also speak to us of the difference between performance and reality, in ways that make them especially useful in
the study of textuality—and in helping us to make sense of our
own lives.

Sacred versus Profane on Screen and Stage in the Twenties

In the first major film to use some spoken dialogue and audible
musical performances, *The Jazz Singer* (1927), sacred and profane
were brought together in an extraordinary way. It is the story of
the son of a Jewish cantor, who takes up popular music instead
of following in his father's footsteps. He runs away from home to
sing on the stage, and finally gets his chance on Broadway, at a moment when his estranged father is near death and wishes to hear
his son sing once more the Aramaic chant for Yom Kippur, the Kol
Nidre, which he had learned as a boy. Torn between performing
the sacred text or singing in blackface to distinctly profane music,
the son, played by Al Jolson, finally manages to sing the sacred
song, easing his father's death and causing the postponement of
his show, though he returns to great success on Broadway. In the
course of the film, we hear parts of the Kol Nidre on three separate
occasions, in addition to a number of popular songs, performed in
clubs and on the stage. But the central character is finally allowed
to have it both ways: to sing the sacred song and then go on to the

profane career that, as we are told, God wants him to have. We may consider this resolution as too easy, but this is an interesting film, set partly in the Jewish ghetto of New York, in scenes that anticipate similar images of the Italian ghetto in *The Godfather II*. The narrative follows closely a short story by Samson Raphaelson, called "The Day of Atonement," which first appeared in *Everybody's Magazine* in 1922. Interestingly enough, this story is itself a fictionalized version of Al Jolson's life. In the world of profane texts, fiction and reality are interwoven in complicated ways, as we shall see.

In *The Jazz Singer* the basic sound track is a pseudoclassical orchestral background, that switches over to "jazz" when the singer performs, and to live dialogue for one important scene, which drew applause from the film's first audience. In musical terms, the film needed a synthesis between the background music and the performance music, but never really attempted it. Such a synthesis between jazz and classical music had already been made by George Gershwin, in *Rhapsody in Blue* (1924), but that was a rare achievement. Gershwin would get his chance to bring this mixture to the stage a few years later, with a play that also caught Al Jolson's interest. In the late 1920s a play about African Americans had a long run on Broadway, leading Jolson to imagine himself playing the lead, in blackface. The play was based on DuBose Heyward's 1926 novel, *Porgy*, and was written by Heyward with the help of his wife, Dorothy, who was a dramatist. Jerome Kern and Oscar Hammerstein were supposed to make a musical out of this story of an African-American community, turning it into a vehicle for Jolson. We should be grateful that this did not happen, because, when this plan fell through, the Heywards turned back to Gershwin, who had been interested in making a "folk opera" of *Porgy* since he first read the novel in 1926. Gershwin had written Heyward about this possibility at that time, but other commitments prevented him from working on it, and he stood aside when Jolson made his bid, because he knew the Heywards needed the money. When Gershwin finally started to work on this project, he spent time in South Carolina with the Heywards, visiting the sites that were prominent in the novel, and then he and his brother Ira began to work on turning *Porgy* into a music drama. Heyward was a poet as well as a novelist, and published frequently in *Poetry* magazine, co-editing, with a friend, an issue of that magazine devoted to southern poetry. In 2002, Stephen Sondheim nominated him for inclusion in a book of biographies called *Invisible Giants*:

> DuBose Heyward has gone largely unrecognized as the author of the finest set of lyrics in the history of the American musical theater—namely, those of *Porgy and Bess*. There are two reasons for this, and they are connected. First, he was primarily a poet and novelist, and his only song lyrics were those that he wrote for *Porgy*. Second, some of them were written in collaboration with Ira Gershwin, a full-time lyricist, whose reputation in the musical theater was firmly established before the opera was written. But most of the lyrics in *Porgy*—and all of the distinguished ones—are by Heyward. I admire his theater songs for their deeply felt poetic style and their insight into character.

That is high praise from a master of musical theatre. George Gershwin's music for *Porgy and Bess* is brilliant—no question. But the words are very important, too, and Sondheim, who writes both words and music for his own plays, knows just how important words can be. Throughout this chapter, we shall be looking at the words and the stories of music dramas, accepting the importance of the music but concentrating on the other textual elements—starting with *Porgy and Bess*.

Sondheim points directly to the connection between musical lyrics and the presentation of character. The main characters in this music drama are Bess and her three lovers: Crown, the brutal stevedore; Porgy, the crippled beggar; and Sportin' Life, the vicious drug dealer. The most profane song in the play, and one of the most memorable—"It Ain't Necessarily So"—is sung by Sportin' Life. In this song he mocks four Old Testament episodes: David's defeat of Goliath, Jonah living inside the whale, the discovery of the baby Moses, and the very long life of Methuselah. What Sportin' Life does not do, however, is mock any of the miraculous events in the New Testament—such as Jesus's walking on water—and there are very good reasons for this. His audience for this song, the inhabitants of Catfish Row at a picnic on Kittiwah Island, would have been outraged if he had mocked that sacred text. The lives of these poor blacks are sustained and made tolerable by the Christianity which is on their lips in speech and song at every turn, and clearly in their hearts and minds as well. This profane text is permeated by the language of sacredness.

Many of the songs in the play are performed out of context in recordings. You can find Ella Fitzgerald singing "It Ain't Necessarily So," for example, as well as "Summertime." One reason for studying *Porgy and Bess* is to recover the context and the meaning of the story, which is no fairy tale but a powerful and disturbing work of naturalism, which persisted through three distinct textual forms: the novel, the stage play, and the music drama that we know. The main events of the story are the same in all three textual forms, though there are interesting changes in the details. Most of these changes were introduced by the Heywards in the stage play, which tightened the structure of the narrative considerably, but Sportin' Life's profane song is pure Gershwin. This is a complex tale, and it will help to see it as two stories—one for each of the title characters of the musical version. Both stories take place in and around Catfish Row, a segregated slum in Charleston, South Carolina. The story of Bess is that of a promiscuous woman dominated by Crown, a powerful brute. She escapes him when he has to flee after murdering a gambler in a drunken rage, and she finds a refuge with the decent Porgy, whom she learns to love. Captured again by Crown, she returns to Porgy in a state of dementia. Rescued from that state by prayer, she begs Porgy to protect her from Crown. But, when Porgy kills Crown to protect Bess and is taken to jail as a "witness," she is seduced by the drug dealer Sportin' Life and heads for New York with him. This is a different ending from that of the novel, in which Bess is taken to Savannah by a gang of stevedores, but it follows the stage play closely.

The story of Porgy is that of a crippled beggar who is feared by the local children, but becomes gentle after he takes in Bess and learns to love her. When he comes back from prison to learn that she has gone to New York with Sportin' Life, he resolves to go and find her, departing on his goat cart (or on crutches in some productions), heading for a city he knows nothing about, on a quest that is certainly doomed, though his song of departure ("Oh Lawd, I'm on my way / I'm on my way, to a Heav'nly land") is distinctly upbeat. The novel ended differently, with Porgy sitting desolate in his wagon, turned into an old man by despair over the loss of Bess. Textual differences of this kind open the way for interpretation and critical judgment, which is a very good reason for bringing them into the classroom.

In all three of its forms, this text was attacked as politically incorrect, though that name for such judgments was not used back in the 1920s and 30s. The reasons for the attacks are understandable. These texts represent life in a black ghetto, in a culture in which white people still dominated absolutely. When a decent white man comes to Catfish Row to help Porgy's jailed friend Peter, the suspicious Porgy asks him, "How you come to care, boss?" And the answer is, "His folks used to belong to my family and I just heard he was in trouble." We are only a few generations from slavery here, in the city where the Civil War began. The poor black people in this community are exploited, oppressed, and find life bearable only through religion—though they also turn to gambling, liquor, and drugs for relief. Still, in all versions of this story, their courage and decency shine through their dire situation, which leads me to reject the view that this text demeans black people. In particular, the language that they use is not, in my view, a debased version of some standard English, but a version that has moved in the direction of poetry, like the speech of the rural Irish in the plays of J. M. Synge. But these questions should certainly be open for discussion in any classroom where these works are considered.

In this short section, I cannot hope to treat these materials with the thoroughness they deserve, but I would like to look at the words of three songs from the music drama as a way of illustrating the interpretive and critical questions they raise. The best-known song in the show is no doubt "Summertime," which combines Gershwin's music with Heyward's lyrics. It is sung on three different occasions: first by Clara, wife of the fisherman Jake, to their baby, in act 1, scene 1; then again by Clara, in act 2, scene 4, before she hands the baby over to Bess and runs out to her death in the raging storm; and, finally, by Bess with Clara's baby, after Jake and Clara's deaths, in act 3, scene 1. This is a beautiful lullaby, but the words are ironic in every instance. The baby being sung to does not have rich parents, and will never open its wings and take to the sky. By the time that Bess sings the song in the last act, this child has no parents at all, and the attempt of Porgy and Bess to act as surrogate parents is clearly doomed.

The second song is sung twice, in slightly different versions. It is "Oh, Doctor Jesus," sung by Serena to cure Bess of her dementia after she has come back to Porgy, and sung by the whole group during the storm that kills Jake and Clara. It is a prayer, really, and it seems to work in the first case, as Bess regains her senses. In the second case, when the prayer is sung by the group during the storm, asking to be saved, some are, and some are not. But both versions are typical of the way that faith in Jesus, in particular, runs through this community, providing hope where earthly things offer little. The first version of this song is especially interesting, because it represents a distinct change from the novel. In the novel, the whole situation is different. Bess is arrested for causing a disturbance and is delirious on her return from jail. But instead of praying to Jesus, the Catfish Row residents send money to a conjure woman for a voodoo cure. The money never reaches her, but Bess recovers, with those around her mistakenly crediting the result to the conjure woman. Both the stage play and the musical version drop the voodoo and emphasize the Christian faith involved—a change that contributes to the coherence and power of the text.

The third important song is "It Ain't Necessarily So." This opera is full of memorable music, with songs like "A Woman Is a Sometime Thing," "I Got Plenty o' Nuttin'," and "Bess, You Is My Woman Now." But Sportin' Life's "It Ain't Necessarily So" is crucial, because it attacks the spirituality that permeates the culture of Catfish Row and its inhabitants. As I indicated above, Sportin' Life avoids attacking Jesus, but he does attack the Bible, and he gets away with it, partly because he catches his audience in a pagan mood, just after they have all sung "I Ain't Got No Shame." It is worth noting that this episode is not in either of the earlier versions, but exists in the music drama alone, where it serves to position its singer as a person who does not belong in this culture. This is a text that grew stronger with every revision. Sportin' Life's unbelief, then, is not a momentary lapse but the essence of his being. He uses the powers of liquor and "happy dust" to earn his living and control others, selling Crown the combination of booze and dope that led to his murderous rage in act 1, and luring Bess away from Porgy with "happy dust" in act 3. He also tries to use loaded dice in the crap game in act 1. He is completely amoral—a Mephistophelian figure who preys on the weak and ignorant, offering his drugs as a replacement for religious faith. New York, as his proper destination, can thus be seen as a kind of hell, to which he is dragging Bess. At the end, when Porgy sings that he is on his way to a heavenly land, he is not really talking about New York City. He and Bess are more likely to rejoin one another in the afterlife than in New York, turning this song into a jazzy version of a *Liebestod*—music in which love and death are inseparable.

This is a bitter story in all its forms, but the music intensifies the ironies. The greatest irony of all, perhaps, is the way that the sacred texts of Christianity function to help the citizens of Catfish Row endure their intolerable situation. This is very clear in the stage version and even clearer in the music drama, because of the way that Sportin' Life's song contrasts with the prevailing values of the culture. In one of the sacred texts of Communism, Karl Marx had this to say about such things: "Religion is the sigh of the oppressed creature, the heart of a heartless world, and the soul of soulless conditions. It is the opium of the people." Those eloquent words might almost foreshadow the world of *Porgy and Bess*, were it not that the people of that world are forced to choose between the metaphorical and the real opium for their consolation, in a world that has added racial discrimination to economic exploitation. Only Heyward's eloquent language and Gershwin's powerful music, reminding us that this is, after all, a text, can make its contemplation a pleasurable experience.

Can't Help It

This phrase comes from the English language version of a song sung by Marlene Dietrich in *The Blue Angel*, one of the first important films of the sound era—produced in 1930 in both German and English versions, and still very much alive. Like *Porgy and Bess*, it was based on a novel. In this case, Heinrich Mann's *Professor Unrat: Das Ende eines Tyrannen* of 1905 was the source, though the film is set in the late 1920s. The title of the novel translates as *Professor Garbage: The End of a Tyrant*, and it is the story of a teacher who bullies his students until he enters into a disastrous marriage with a cabaret performer and loses his job. His real name is not Unrat, which means trash, rubbish, or garbage. That is just the nickname his rebellious students have given him because his name sounds like that. In the book, translated in 1944 as *Small Town Tyrant*, his savings are eaten up by his marriage to the performer, Rosa Frölich, and he turns their house into a gambling den. Trying to maintain an exalted position in the town, he runs up huge debts which he refuses to pay, while Rosa slips away regularly to entertain other men: "Yet she was grateful to him for playing his part in the comedy, since her now daily lapses meant so much to him still. But it did make a performance of Life! Funny that he never seemed to get accustomed to it!" In the end the professor tries to strangle Rosa, and steals the pocketbook of a former student, leading to the arrest of both of them. The novel ends with their being put in a police car—the tyrant deposed at last.

The film makes interesting changes in this story, but the most important is that, instead of turning his house into a gambling den to earn his keep, the professor begins to perform as a clown in the show, ultimately returning to the town where he used to teach, and going crazy as his former students and others laugh at his pathetic performance. Often, films made from novels are disappointing, but sometimes, as in *The Man Who Shot Liberty Valance*, they actually improve on the original. In *The Blue Angel*, having the professor perform as a clown gives the story a tighter and more dramatic structure, and Heinrich Mann approved of von Sternberg's changes, saying that he wished he had thought of the film's ending when he wrote the novel. This is an excellent opportunity for comparative textuality, using the novel and film as ways into the intentions of the makers, and for critical judgment.

There is a very useful volume called *The Blue Angel*, published to mark the fiftieth anniversary of the film's production, which has a second translation of Mann's novel (in which the professor's nickname is "Mud"), along with the English version of the screenplay and some interesting comments by von Sternberg on the changes he made and the reasons for them. Students should have access to this volume, or, at the very least, von Sternberg's commentary should be made available to them. In the film version the professor ends by madly fleeing the stage and sneaking into his former school, where he clings to his old desk in his madness. The role of the clown, which runs from Shakespeare to Sondheim, looms very large in performance texts, and it has interesting connections to the role of the teacher, which is another kind of performance, though we don't always like to acknowledge that. But this film suggests that the extremes of teaching may be defined by clowning and tyranny—and that both are roles. This is emphasized by the contrast between the professor alone in his home and in his classroom. We see him in his own rooms, sensitively dealing with the death of his little canary, and we see him in his regimented classroom, trying to play the tyrant, but it is clear that he is performing in his role of teacher, paving the way for his other performances.

The film does not merely change the story by making the professor less of a tyrant and more sympathetic. It also adds images and music to this changed tale, and both are interesting. The external scenes have a surreal quality, showing us a world like that of the silent expressionist film *The Cabinet of Dr. Caligari*, produced just a decade earlier. But the internal scenes are packed with people who look strange but real. In art-historical terms, we are moving, here, from expressionism to what was called "New Objectivity" (*Neue Sachlichkeit*)—a kind of exaggerated naturalism exemplified by painters like Otto Dix and Max Beckmann in the period after World War I. The "Blue Angel" is a cabaret, which becomes the scene of the crucial events in the film that bears its name. It is a small-town predecessor of the Berlin cabarets of the 1930s, made famous by Christopher Isherwood's novels and the play and film made from them, ultimately called *Cabaret*.

Both these films and their antecedent versions can profitably be studied together, but we are concentrating on the early film here, because it introduced one of the most famous musical scenes in film history: Marlene Dietrich singing the song we know as "Falling in Love Again." The original German is rather different: *Ich bin von Kopf bis Fuß auf Liebe eingestellt* (I am, from head to foot, ready for love). The English version goes this way: "Falling in love again. / Never wanted to. / What am I to do? / Can't help it." It is, in English, a song about being helpless in the grip of an emotion. But, as Dietrich performs it, the character Lola-Lola, who is singing in the cabaret, is clearly not helpless before emotion. She is a professional who performs and sells emotion—or the semblance of it. And she is totally in control of the stage and the audience, ordering a fellow performer to get up and give her a chair during her performance, and bewitching the watching professor with it as well.

This is the great scene in the film, partly because of the way Dietrich acts and sings, but also because of the performance of Emil Jannings in the role of the professor, with his emotions readable on his face and through his posture and gestures. We are not far from silent films here. Unlike the tyrant of the novel, he is really an innocent. But this scene is also interesting because of the way the cinematic text is arranged. As Dietrich/Lola sings, the camera cuts back and forth from her on the stage to the professor in a special balcony seat, gazing at her. He is clearly falling in love and can't help it. He has just been introduced to the cabaret audience as a distinguished guest in a special box seat, so that he is on something like a stage of his own, with others watching him as he watches her, growing more and more bemused as her song goes on. This, then, is a performance about performance—about a spectator being captured by a deceptive actress and being drawn toward performing himself.

In the film, that becomes the story of his life. There is a sad clown visible in most of the cabaret interiors in the first part of the film. But when the professor runs out of money after some years of living with Lola-Lola and must perform to earn his keep, the role given him is that of the clown, who becomes the butt of the stage magician's jokes, with pigeons coming out of his hat and eggs being pulled out of his nose, leading him to crow like a rooster. What ultimately drives him over the edge of sanity into madness is being brought back to his old town to perform, before an audience that includes the former students he used to tyrannize, and being forced to enact his role as clown there, in the Blue Angel, while Lola-Lola flirts with another performer. This scene, too, is powerfully performed by Jannings.

The book was about the professor, and so, in terms of billing and screen time, was the film, but Dietrich stole it. It has become her film—because of the music and her memorable performance of it, which has been imitated by all sorts of singers, all over the world. It is a film, then, about the power of performance, and about the unequal struggle between the tyranny of the classroom and the manipulative magic of the stage. It is about the victory of feeling over thought and the power of false feeling over real emotions, making it a cautionary tale for all students of textuality. The viewer sees both the character Lola-Lola performing and the actress Marlene Dietrich performing, and the combination is extraordinarily seductive. We can't help but fall a bit in love with this performance, I believe, but we should not make the mistake of loving the fictional character or the real actress who played her so unforgettably. We can help that.

Nobody's Perfect

These words are the last spoken in a film, though they might be the motto of this book. In the film they are uttered by an aging roué upon being told that the woman he wants to marry is actually a man. These words might seem utterly inadequate to the situation—an imperfect utterance about an imperfect situation in an imperfect cinematic text—but they also convey an opposed significance, an acceptance of imperfection as the human condition, reducing the difference in gender to another aspect of a very original sin. If Adam had been perfect, he wouldn't have needed Eve. Sexual differentiation and all its attendant forms of imperfection were already in Paradise—put there by the God who created the need for sexual difference and required Noah to bring two of everything aboard the ark. "Imperfect" means "unfinished," and that is what Adam was before Eve, who made his imperfection official and helped him finish living in what he had thought was Paradise. The words of the roué also suggest, however, that gender itself is a performance, which is a major theme in this movie.

The film closed by the words "nobody's perfect" is *Some Like It Hot*, a comedy about performance, about playing roles and getting stuck in them to some extent. The two main male characters are musicians named Joe and Jerry, who become witnesses to a mob killing on St. Valentine's Day in Chicago, in 1929. There was a real massacre on that date in Chicago, with an Italian gang killing members of a rival Irish group, and this fictional film includes a version of that crime. We first see Joe and Jerry playing in a band in a speakeasy disguised as a funeral parlor. Later, by accident, they witness the massacre and are seen by the killers, forcing them to get out of town any way they can. The only way turns out to be disguised as members of an all-girl jazz band, The Sweet Sues, who are leaving Chicago for an engagement at a beach hotel in Florida. So our two "heroes" must become female, which, among other things, allows them to see things from the perspective of the women, who are always getting hit on by all sorts of men. The lead singer of the band, Sugar, played by Marilyn Monroe, has had a lot of experience with that, and hopes to escape it by finding a rich man to marry in Florida.

Things get more complicated when Joe (now "Josephine") falls in love with Sugar and keeps sneaking out of his female persona and playing the role of a male millionaire in order to woo her. In this guise, he speaks almost exactly like Cary Grant—so there are roles within roles in this performance. He also pretends to be frigid, leading Sugar to try to awaken his desire, while they are both alone on an actual millionaire's yacht. The spectacle of Marilyn Monroe trying to awaken the sexual instinct of a man is hilarious, with the reclining man's leg going up in the air while he pretends not to be stirred by her kisses. At the same moment, the actual owner of the yacht is dancing with "Daphne," the female character being performed by Jerry, in a nightclub ashore, so that the camera keeps cutting back and forth between the two bizarre love scenes. By the end of the evening, Sugar and Joe are really in love, and Jerry has actually had a very good time dancing with the millionaire, Osgood Fielding, who has proposed to him in his role as Daphne. Back in his hotel room, Jerry is still dancing, reenacting the pleasures of the evening.

Music functions in the film in various ways. If we compare this film to *The Blue Angel*, which is set at almost the same moment in history, the character of Sugar plays a similar role to that of Lola-Lola in the German film, and the two actresses, Dietrich and Monroe, are certainly icons of sexuality. But Sugar is herself a kind of innocent. She, too, sings of love, but her song is "I Wanna Be Loved by You," with a childish Boop-boop-a-doo as a refrain—a song of 1928, which inspired the cartoon character, Betty Boop. In actuality, if such a word can be used about this fictional world, Sugar does keep "falling in love again"—with saxophone players who treat her badly. Apparently, she "can't help it." But she doesn't sing Dietrich's song, or anything quite like it, though she does rehearse "Runnin' Wild" with the band. Her childish ambition is to marry a rich man with a yacht, but when her millionaire turns out to be just another saxophone player, she doesn't reject him. *Some Like It Hot* was actually inspired by a German musical film of 1951, called *Fanfaren der Liebe* (Fanfares of Love), but it goes its own American way of "screwball comedy." This is another case, however, where the differences can be profitably investigated. (The German film is hard to locate, but interesting information about it is available online.)

Another function of music in *Some Like It Hot* is as a kind of social marker. When Sugar first encounters Jerry, in his millionaire costume and Cary Grant accent, they talk about different kinds of music, and Jerry says, "I prefer classical, but some like it hot," giving the film its title. And when the Chicago gangsters turn up at the same Florida hotel as the jazz band, it is to meet other mafia types at what is supposed to be a gathering of "Friends of Italian Opera," but is actually just a meeting of Italian gangsters who have it in for one another. The leader of the Chicago group offers, as his alibi for that massacre, his supposed attendance at a performance of *Rigoletto*, but one of his sidekicks thinks he is claiming to have been at a joint called Rigoletto's. (Verdi's opera of that name is about a clown called Rigoletto and a Duke who disguises himself as a student in order to woo and win a young woman who turns out to be Rigoletto's daughter—which leads the clown to plead with the Duke's courtiers to help him find her, in an aria we will encounter in the next section of this chapter.) But this meeting of Italian opera lovers in *Some Like It Hot* turns out to be just an occasion for a Florida encore of the Chicago massacre, witnessed again by our hapless musicians, leading to another flight by them and, ultimately, to the abandonment of the roles they have been playing. This time, they escape on a boat headed to Fielding's yacht, with Sugar on board and Fielding dismissing all Jerry's arguments against their marriage, including Jerry's actual gender, with the words "nobody's perfect."

All this role playing and its attendant interpretive conundrums should remind us that the concept of fiction itself has a history. Jonathan Rose has actually traced modes of working-class reading in the eighteenth and nineteenth centuries. What he discovered is that most of the early working-class readers who have left evidence of how they read actually lacked the concept of fiction. The most popular texts in this world were the Bible, *Pilgrim's Progress*, and *Robinson Crusoe*—and these readers took them all to be literally true. That is, the sacred text, the allegorical tale, and the pseudo-document were all accorded the same interpretive status by people just moving into the world of books in the eighteenth century.

We need to be reminded, perhaps, that sophistication about fact and fiction in narrative comes only with the attainment of a similar sophistication in the world of the physical sciences. The rise of the realistic novel accompanies the rise of the empirical sciences in Europe. Art and science are concepts that depend on one another. And both notions are involved in the idea of fiction, which is a crucial tool in textual studies, enabling us to see levels and modes of truth and lies in texts. Texts that proclaim their truth are never entirely truthful, and those that insist that they are lies are often lying about that, too. *The Jazz Singer* is, at some level, actually about Al Jolson, who is playing the role of Jack Robin in the film. And the character Porgy was based on a real beggar known as "Goat-Sammy" Smalls, who was afterward remembered only as Porgy. Singers may be playing entirely false roles in their songs—or actually revealing things about themselves while performing. Even this delightfully absurd comedy, *Some Like It Hot*, is grounded in a very real Chicago massacre that took place on the day of lovers—St. Valentine's. What students may learn, then, when they study textuality, is how imperfect beings may navigate through imperfect texts, interpreting and criticizing the different levels of deceit and truthfulness inscribed in those texts. I hope I have made it plain, by now, that these skills are needed, and that teachers of English must do their best to help their students develop them.

I've Become Lost to the World

You may think I have become lost myself, for I want to begin here with a poem in German, written by Friedrich Rückert in the 1840s. Rückert was a professor of Oriental languages and a poet whose poems have been set to music by such composers as Schubert, the Schumanns, Brahms, Mahler, Richard Strauss, Zemlinsky, Hindemith, Bartók, Berg, and Wolf. I am introducing this poem as a way of considering how a verbal text can become part of a musical text and then how both can become part of a cinematic text—with a result that combines the powers of all these media into a version of the total work of art envisioned by Richard Wagner. Here is the poem, then, with a line-by-line translation.

Ich bin der Welt abhanden gekommen,	(I've become lost to the world,)
mit der ich sonst viele Zeit verdorben,	(where I used to waste so much time,)
sie hat so lange nichts von mir vernommen,	(it hasn't heard from me in so long,)
sie mag wohl glauben, ich sei gestorben!	(that it may well think I am dead!)
Es ist mir auch gar nichts daran gelegen,	(For me it does not matter at all,)
ob sie mich für gestorben hält,	(if it considers me dead,)
ich kann auch gar nichts sagen dagegen,	(I can say nothing at all against this,)
denn wirklich bin ich gestorben der Welt.	(since I am really dead to the world.)
Ich bin gestorben dem Weltgetümmel,	(I am dead to the world's tumult,)
und ruh' in einem stillen Gebiet!	(and rest in a quiet place!)
Ich leb' allein in meinem Himmel,	(I live alone in my heaven,)
in meinem Lieben, in meinem Lied!	(in my love, in my song!)

Half a century or so after its composition this poem was set to music by Gustav Mahler, and this version has been sung by many notable performers since then. Recordings of it are widely available. I would recommend the one by Janet Baker with John Barbirolli conducting on EMI Records, but there are many good ones from which to choose. Mahler set a number of Rückert's poems, collectively known as the *Rückertlieder* (Rückert songs), and they are among his finest works. His setting of "I've become lost to the world" is usually considered his best, and he said of it, "it is truly me" (as the notes to the Baker performance tell us, drawing on Natalie Bauer-Lechner's *Recollections of Gustav Mahler*). We can start by trying to understand the poem.

The situation is quite simple. The speaker is apparently alive but living in retirement, out of the "world" and away from worldly concerns—living "in my love, in my song"—and he claims that this retired life is like being in heaven. But the speaker is alone in that heaven, with his love and his song. If we assume that the speaker is the poet or a persona of the poet, as the phrase "my song" suggests, we must note that being alone in love does not sound like the happiest of situations. There is a bittersweet quality to the poem which is a major source of its interest. There is a pull between joy and sorrow here. Even in Paradise, Adam did not like being alone. And this speaker has known love as Adam had not. The "song" is the last thing mentioned, the climax of the poem, however, and it is presented as the major joy in this lonely life in heaven. The ability to "sing," to make music with words, is what makes being dead to the world a situation that can be called heavenly.

If we see the words as those of the poet Rückert, we cannot help but note that he is now really dead, living only in the words of the song that he has left us. If we read the words as those of the composer Mahler, who gave those words a lovely orchestral setting, thinking about himself as he composed, the word *song* becomes more literal. This has indeed become Mahler's *Lied*. And because it is a song, it can be sung—and is sung—by voices all along the musical scale, by men and women, all of whom, at the moment of singing, are entitled to think "it is truly me," even though they may be far from living in retirement as they sing. The poem provides a role to be performed, a role for which music could be written, as Mahler wrote it, so that it is frequently sung or performed by opera singers. Mahler wrote no operas, but he wrote for the voice a lot and we should all be grateful for that, since his music is wonderfully expressive. Mahler, too, is dead now, but alive and in his heaven whenever his song is performed. This song has gone places he might not have envisioned, however, and one of those places is what I wish to explore next.

In 1988 a film called *Le Maître de Musique* was released, having been directed in Belgium by Gérard Corbiau, with the title usually given in English as *The Music Teacher*. A good deal is lost in that apparently simple translation of the title, but the film is indeed about teaching, which makes it relevant to our concerns in more than one way. When the film opens, the master of music in question is a singer who is performing in a British concert hall at the beginning of the twentieth century, singing an aria from Verdi's *Rigoletto*, in which the court jester asks the Duke's courtiers for pity. He hesitates for a moment in completing his performance, possibly in pain, and then announces at the end that he is retiring from public singing. This singer, Joachim Dallayrac, is played by the well-known opera bass-baritone José van Dam. He retires to an elegant estate in the country, where he lives with his accompanist, Estelle, and in his retirement he takes on two pupils: a young woman who is the niece of a friend of his, and a young man he rescues from a career of petty thievery, after Dallayrac hears him singing an aria from Offenbach's *Tales of Hoffmann* while picking a pocket.

We see the master's teaching methods in some detail. He is extremely demanding and persistent, treating both the mental and physical aspects of singing with great care. He is definitely a master and not just a teacher in this role. He is also dying and experiencing occasional moments of debilitating pain. The master and his students are locked in emotional relationships that are intense, involving gratitude and rebellion, and, in the case of the young woman, something like love. We see her and her teacher at one point, riding in a carriage, singing music from *Don Giovanni* in which the Don woos a young woman who admits that she wants and doesn't want to yield to him ("Vorrei e non vorrei"). And we see the young man, swimming behind the teacher, who is rowing away from him on the estate's small lake, forcing him to develop his lungs and breath control. We also see the young man stomping out of a lesson in anger and fiercely chopping wood to work off his rage. And we see the young woman walking away from her teacher in a rainstorm, because he is not Don Giovanni after all, and will not become her lover, though he feels something like love for her.

Images of the changing seasons tell us that years are passing, though we do not know exactly how many have passed when the two young students are invited to a singing contest by a former rival of their teacher. Dallayrac has them driven to the palatial home of that former rival, Prince Scotti, but leaves them there and goes back in his carriage alone. On the way there, however, we hear on the sound track the opening lines of Mahler's setting of Rückert's poem sung by Van Dam. Music, then, has two functions in this film. We see and hear it performed, but we also hear it when no performance is taking place, as a commentary or reflection on the situations that we see. In this case, what we are seeing is the beginning of the end of Joachim Dallayrac. This music may or may not be in his mind, as the carriage rides on, but it is certainly brought into *our* minds as we listen to it. In any case, the performance is not completed during this ride, and Dallayrac returns home, leaving his pupils to their fate in the contest. They do well, because they have learned from a master teacher, and because they have bonded and support one another emotionally and musically during the contest, despite Prince Scotti's attempts to manipulate the result in favor of his own pupil.

At certain moments during the contest, however, we move back to Dallayrac's villa, where he has returned to the arms of his accompanist, Estelle. At one point, he moves to the piano and accompanies himself, singing Schubert's lovely song "An die Musik," an ode to music, with verses written by Schubert's friend Franz von Schober, in which the speaker thanks the "gracious art" (*holde Kunst*) for often taking him to "a better world" (*eine bessere Welt*). This is the last thing we hear Dallayrac sing while alive—but not the last time we hear Van Dam's voice singing in the film. After singing "An die Musik," Dallayrac dies quietly in a chair, dropping his coffee cup. Just after his pupils have triumphed at the contest, however, they are notified of their teacher's death and set out to return to his villa at once. And then some complex cinematic things happen. We see the young singers sitting in a carriage, and we begin to hear the last quatrain of Mahler's setting of Rückert's poem, sung by Van Dam—or Dallayrac—and then, with the song continuing, we cut away from the carriage to a scene in which the body of Dallayrac is being transported across the little lake, away from the villa where he died and toward its place of interment.

Estelle is standing and watching in mourning garments, and she is joined there by the young singers, Sophie and Jean, as we hear the final lines of the song: "I live alone in my heaven, in my love, in my song." In the poem, the speaker is in some rural retreat from the bustle of "the world," but who is singing these words? Dallayrac is dead—in a literal heaven, perhaps, but not a figurative one—but he seems to be having a final word here. But when he sings the phrase "Ich leb' allein" (I live alone), the camera gives us a close-up of Estelle, who then whispers to Sophie that she now wants time to pass quickly. She is alone, and far from heaven, but the whisper makes it seem as if she is hearing what we are hearing, and her whispered words resonate ironically with the words of the song, just as the image of her solitude does. Mahler's version of the poem repeats the line "with my love," which is especially appropriate for this moment in the film, with Dallayrac's two loves, Estelle and Sophie, standing together watching his body move away from them out on the lake. Without getting too technical, we can note that, at this point in the song, the music rises for heaven and the first love, but descends with the second and moves down through the major chord of the song's key to a final point of calm at the word *song* (*Lied*)—which is especially effective in the deep voice of Van Dam. At this point, we cut away from the funereal lake, leaving Estelle alone, and return to the same carriage we were in before, with the two young people whose solemnity is now touched with the faintest hints of joy, as they escape from the master of music and go out toward their own futures.

When we first see them in that carriage we undoubtedly think that Sophie and Jean are going back toward death and burial, but when we see them again, after the Mahler and the boats being poled across the lake with the body draped in white, we realize that this scene actually comes after the funeral, so that these young singers are headed not toward death but toward life, and that in their lives the master of music will also live, because of what they have learned from him, and because music has almost magical powers to transform the lives of those who devote themselves to it, whether as composers or interpreters of that "gracious art." Dallayrac's voice, accompanying his dead body as it crosses the water, lives on in the minds of the three people who are watching from the shore and in the minds of those who hear it on the sound track of the film. He sang his farewell when alive, using Schubert's song, and then sings an encore after death, using Mahler's. This is a film, then, about the power of an art that combines words and music, presented in a form that adds images to that already powerful mixture, and it is a film about the power of teaching as well, and the transcendental joy that it can bring to those who do it well. It is not a great film, perhaps, but it is a powerful and beautiful one, especially for those of us who love poetry, music, film, or teaching—or all of the above.

The Pleasurable Pains of Opera

Here I must warn the reader that we are going to take a rather deep plunge into the world of opera in this section. I think it will be useful, but, if it is too heavy, please just hop to the next section, which will be lighter. (You can always come back.)

At the end of chapter 2 we encountered Rebecca West's defense of opera, in which she raised this question: "Can you say that a bomb which might have blown you to smithereens matters less than a song supposed to be sung by a lady's maid, who, however, never existed, when waiting for the embraces of a valet, who, also, never existed?" Her answer was "Yes," that we need the kind of emotional empathy and release that the hyper-fictional medium of opera provides. This defense itself comes in that very profane text, *Black Lamb and Grey Falcon*, a work of journalism rather than literature which is nevertheless very literary and worth studying for many reasons. Following her lead, it is time now to look more deeply into just what operatic texts accomplish if we "read" them as well as hear them. As we have noted in considering *Porgy and Bess* and *Le Maître de Musique*, it is not always easy to distinguish between song and opera, since operas are full of songs and songs can have operatic dimensions, including full orchestral scores and dramatic situations. Words have power. Music has power. Images have power. Performance has power. Combine them all effectively and you will have something very powerful indeed.

But power is not the only thing that these mixed media can provide. They can also provide food for thought. And even this most profane medium, opera, can direct our attention usefully to matters that are usually the domain of sacred texts. In this section, then, I want to discuss opera as a medium that mixes pleasure and pain in complicated ways, and can do the same thing with thought and feeling. We can begin by considering the following painful occasions for song in a number of operas:

A woman fends off a rapist/seducer only to find that he has killed her father on his way out of her bedroom. Reduced to sobs at the occasion "Quel sangue . . . Quel piaga . . . Quel volto" (This blood, this wound, this face), she later recounts the event and sings powerfully of honor and revenge in a famous aria— "Or sai chi l'onore." (*Don Giovanni*)

An old man is thrown into a laundry basket and dumped into the river Thames, and then mocked brutally when he survives the river. His response is to observe that everything in the world is a joke and the people only clowns—"Tutto nel mondo è burla." (*Falstaff*)

Considering her husband's inattention and infidelities, a woman asks where her past life has gone, where her young self may be, in a famous aria—"Dove sono."(*Le Nozze di Figaro*)

Despairing and having just joined the army in desperation, a lover takes some pleasure in a furtive tear from his beloved— "Una furtiva lagrima." (*L'elisir d'amore*)

Worried about losing her young lover and growing old, a woman sings about her painful awareness of the strangeness of time—"Die Zeit, die ist ein sonderbar Ding."(*Der Rosenkavalier*)

Having just become engaged to a beautiful woman, a young man finds another man descending from her bedroom and wishes he were blind and deaf—"Ich müsste blind sein."(*Arabella*)

And that's just the comedies! The more serious operas are full of suffering. Puccini alone gives us two horrific scenes of torture— including one in which the lover of the tortured man has to listen to his cries of anguish—in addition to the suffering of a woman abandoned in the deserts of Louisiana, the anguish of friends around the bedside of a young woman dying of tuberculosis, and the ritualized suicide of a woman betrayed by a feckless naval officer. If we start on Verdi, there's no stopping—in fact the weeping goes on steadily ("Piangi, piangi") throughout his oeuvre. As it does through those of Bellini, Donizetti, Berlioz, Wagner, Gounod, Tchaikovsky, Bizet, Massenet, and Janácek as well, crossing national and linguistic barriers with ease. And these people sing while they are suffering and when they are dying, whether from fatal illness or mortal wounds. It's a strange medium, opera—none stranger.

I got interested in it because I had this girlfriend who assumed that a civilized person would know about opera. Not wanting her to discover just how uncivilized I was, I started hanging out in the local record store, where I usually went to hear jazz records, now listening to arias on the old 78-rpm records, and fending off guys who kept trying to pick me up. I also bought some operatic records, when I could afford to, and listened to them. Without knowing any of the stories or understanding any of the languages, I was moved by what I heard and began to distinguish between an adequate and a brilliant rendition of the same aria. (And, yes, dear reader, I married the girl.) It took years, however, (and another marriage, another life) before I found the time to really learn something about the history of the medium, to learn a bit of some languages, to understand what was actually going on in most of the operas in the standard repertory, and to bring these resources into my teaching. But the pleasure was there before I could connect words and stories to the music, and it didn't diminish as my knowledge expanded, though it changed in quality, as Schiller would put it, from naïve to sentimental. Anyone who likes music—of any kind—can learn to enjoy opera. I am certain that listening to Louis Armstrong, Billie Holliday, and even Al Jolson, prepared me to deal with opera.

One of the things I learned when I got serious about the medium was that opera had functioned for almost two centuries before the voices of women began to be heard on the stage. Until the latter part of the eighteenth century that void was filled by another, with all roles for the highest voices being sung by castrati, former boy sopranos who made a great sacrifice to remain sopranos, though no longer boys. But when female singers began to flourish and composers began to write for their voices, opera entered into its major phase as a cultural force—and this, I submit, is no coincidence. In Shakespeare's day, which was also the time when opera first began to be performed, the roles of women were played by young men on the stage, which is why Cleopatra (in *Antony and Cleopatra*) muses about a future in which some boy will perform her on the stage. What Cleopatra could not imagine, because she could see no further than Shakespeare's own time, was that Berlioz would compose a brilliant version of her final scene for female voice and orchestra—but that happened.

The opening of the theatre and operatic stage to women changed many things, and I believe that some of the performances that resulted helped certain cultures to transcend the limitations put on women by sacred texts, as composers began to generate roles for women that showed them as capable of more than passive suffering. It is not the case that all female singers have voices that are soft in tone and high in pitch. I have a recording of a scene from Verdi's *Ernani* in which the hero and heroine are sung by Pavarotti and Joan Sutherland, while the role of Don Ruy Gomez de Silva, written for a male basso, is sung by Marilyn Horne. But Horne is not your typical mezzo-soprano. Female voices can and often do provide a warmth of tone and a range of emotional coloring that male voices seldom reach. And composers began writing for those voices toward the end of the eighteenth century, quickly extending the roles for women singers from female characters to boys and young men like Cherubino in Mozart's opera about Figaro's wedding.

In the remainder of this section, I want to suggest that we can trace a broad change in the relation of these roles to operatic pain during the century and a half following *Le Nozze di Figaro*, a change that has had an important cultural impact on the roles played by women in actual life. My argument will necessarily be schematic and overly simple, perhaps grossly so. But here it is. The suitability of female characters for the role of victims in plots of melodramatic action was clearly apparent to the composers of those Romantic productions that we know as the "bel canto" operas of the early nineteenth century. From Bellini, Donizetti, and the early Verdi we have a parade of lovely, tender victims of male brutality and oppression, with names like Beatrice, Lucia, Violetta, and Gilda. But even in these operas some female characters have a dignity and strength of purpose that raises them above the level of mere victims. Bellini's Druid priestess Norma is a case in point. There were seeds here of something that flourished later in the century.

Richard Wagner, for example, admired Bellini, transcribed some of his work for piano and even wrote a cavatina for insertion into Bellini's *Il Pirata*. And Wagner is a key figure in the historical narrative I am proposing. Wagner also admired Beethoven, and Beethoven's only opera, *Fidelio*, provided a model of female strength that was not lost on the admiring Wagner. In that opera, it is the "hero," Florestan, who is languishing helplessly, unjustly imprisoned, until his wife, Leonora, comes to the rescue, facing down the villain at the point of her gun, when he comes to murder her vulnerable husband. "Mein Engel Leonora," sings Florestan, and she is a gun-totin' angel indeed. What I think Wagner learned from Beethoven and Bellini was that a female character who combined vulnerability with real strength could be the central figure of a *Gesamtkunstwerk*, a total work of operatic art. And he gave us such a character in Brünnhilde, whom I want to situate as the pivotal figure in my narrative as well as in Wagner's *Ring des Nibelungen*.

Wagner's *Ring* is a sequence of four operas in which Wagner presents the story of the end of the mythic reign of Norse gods and their heroic puppets, one of whom, Siegfried, rises against them, leading to their eclipse in the fourth opera, *The Twilight of the Gods*, or *Götterdämmerung*. The implications of this narrative were drawn out by Bernard Shaw in his *Perfect Wagnerite* and embodied in a Bayreuth production of the opera (available on video), which ended with the chorus turning and staring into the audience. This chorus was reminding the audience that, since the gods are gone, it will be necessary for humans to work out their own destiny from this point on. This new dispensation has certain parallels with the shift from the Old Testament to the New Testament in Christian teaching, including one that is especially important for my purposes here. The major figure in the *Ring* is not Wotan, the leader of the gods, nor any of his male progeny. It is his daughter Brünnhilde, who makes exactly the same sacrifice that Jesus makes in the Christian story, taking on human flesh and ultimately dying for the sins of others, thus connecting this worldly entertainment to the most sacred text in our culture. It is Brünnhilde who begins the decline of the gods in the second opera of the series, *Die Walküre,* by allowing Sieglinde to escape from Wotan; it is Brünnhilde who dominates the end of the third opera, *Siegfried*, with her awakening to human life; and it is Brünnhilde, in the final *Götterdämmerung*, who rides into her funeral pyre on her horse, Grane, returning the ring to the Rhine Maidens, as Valhalla, the home of the old gods, goes up in flames.

But we must look at Brünnhilde's story in greater detail to understand it properly. She is Wotan's favorite child, the leader of his nine Walkyrie daughters, the one who urges him to stand up to his wife and not let his adulterous guilt lead him to betray his human favorites. And when he sends her to bring the soul of Siegmund to the heaven of heroes in Valhalla, she tries to do his bidding. Approaching Siegmund, she offers him a hero's heavenly reward. He asks her if his beloved sister and lover, Sieglinde, will go with him to Valhalla, and, when he learns that this heaven is an exclusively

male club, he rejects the offer. Brünnhilde is so moved by this human love that she betrays Wotan and refuses to carry out his orders.
Fleeing with Sieglinde and her unborn child, Brünnhilde is caught
by Wotan and punished, but Sieglinde escapes. (Between this opera
and the next, Sieglinde dies in childbirth, but her son, Siegfried,
survives.) Interestingly enough, Brünnhilde's punishment for having defied Wotan is to lose her status as a chaste goddess and be
forced to marry the first man who finds her. Marriage to a man
as punishment! Makes you wonder what Wagner was thinking
about, doesn't it? But Brünnhilde strikes a bargain with her father
and is put to sleep in a place surrounded by fires that only a hero
will have the courage to penetrate. Unfortunately, heroes turn out
to be no better husbands than ordinary men.

As it happens, when that hero penetrates the flames and wakes
Brünnhilde from her magical sleep at the end of the third opera in
the *Ring* sequence, he turns out to be the child whose life she had
saved, the offspring of an incestuous love, who is about to take as
his wife a woman who has had maternal feelings about him, and is,
in a sense his godmother, or goddess-mother. This is a profane text
in more ways than one. But the awakening of Brünnhilde, and her
gradual acceptance of being both a human and a wife generate the
most powerful scene in the opera. (It also makes one think about
what Christianity might have been like if Jesus had been required
to marry, but that's another story.) Marriage, however, just begins
Brünnhilde's pains. Her young husband goes off a-heroing and
falls in with evil companions, who drug his drink and make him
forget he is married, so that he marries into their tribe. Then they
kill him. After which Brünnhilde arrives for revenge, which she
exacts, forgiving the hapless boy, Siegfried, and starting the fire
which will consume Valhalla, the home of the gods, and end their
reign—a fire into which she rides, heroic to the end.

My point here is that Brünnhilde is not the pathetic victim in a
melodramatic plot like the heroines of the bel canto operas but an

entirely tragic figure, whose flaw is being moved by human love to lose her pitiless divinity and take on human flesh herself. In this she parallels that only begotten child of the Christian God who became a victim of human cruelty and suffered a painful death before rising to heaven again. But, in Brünnhilde's case, she refused to be a passive victim and she brought about the fated end of her father's reign and of the old dispensation of gods and heroes. Wagner's Brünnhilde, and his Isolde, who resembles Brünnhilde in certain ways, had a profound influence on later operas, to the extent that even those roles that seem to be made for melodramatic victims often have a more heroic aspect. For example, Cio-Cio-San, in Puccini's *Madama Butterfly*, using her disgraced father's ceremonial sword to take her own life, is not, at that moment, a weak figure, but a heroine restoring the family honor, a victim refusing to be pathetic. And Tosca, pursued by police and leaping to her death from the top of the Castel Sant' Angelo after the death of her lover, believes she is going to an appointment "before God" with the villain Scarpia, whom she had killed when he tried to force himself on her. We still have our consumptive Mimìs and our pathetic Manons ("Sola, perduta, abbandonata"—alone, lost, abandoned), but operatic pain changed in the later nineteenth century. I believe Nietzsche had something to do with this—or perhaps his friend Lou Salomé, who posed for a photograph with a whip beating *him*. Nietzsche admired Bizet's *Carmen*, which is an opera about a woman who feels free to change lovers whenever she wants to and is prepared to pay a tragic price for that freedom, becoming an ancestor of Lola-Lola in *The Blue Angel*, though Lola-Lola, in modernist Berlin, gets away with it.

In his brilliant book *In Search of Wagner*, Theodor Adorno laments the fact that Wagner pushed music in the direction of film and the vulgar stage, with detachable units in his operas that could become commodities and be performed anywhere, because they already were commodified in the detestable bourgeois world in which Wagner lived and composed. It is a powerful book, but it never quite acknowledges that history has taken humanity through many worse worlds than the bourgeois nineteenth century and may yet lead us to more of them. Adorno's reading of Wagner depends too much on the sacred texts of Marxism for my taste. I am a bourgeois—or perhaps that is a role I learned to play to please my parents, who had climbed into that class from below, so that now I find myself stuck in that performance. For me, and for anyone who knows the full texts, the detachable songs and arias of music drama bring the whole works to life around them whenever they are performed, providing us with perspectives on the reality in which we live. When I first heard the snippets of opera, I could not make that move, because I really was uncultured. One of the things learning about opera enabled me to discover is that culture is a doorway to pleasure—not the only one, certainly, but a real one. Learning something about the history of art makes every work of art more interesting. And learning about music drama allows us not only to position individual songs or arias in the works from which they have been drawn, but also to make connections from work to work, and every such connection increases both our understanding and our pleasure.

The most direct descendants of Wagner's Brünnhilde and Isolde, and the most Nietzschean of operatic heroines, are the Salome and Elektra of Richard Strauss. Strauss's *Salome* is based on Oscar Wilde's play and follows the play closely. This disconcerting heroine first subjects John the Baptist to her erotic gaze, praising his skin, his hair, and his mouth, before demanding his head as the price of her own submission to the erotic gaze of King Herod. And she sings her way to her own death, triumphing over the fetishized head of the dead saint, "Ich habe deinen Mund geküsst, Jochanaan" (I have kissed your mouth, John). This is another *Liebestod* or love-death, like the one that ends *Tristan und Isolde*, and in it pain and pleasure are interwoven with madness and lust. Something similar happens at the end of *Elektra* as well, when Elektra, who has been a victim and suffered badly, rejoices in the vengeance imposed upon her mother and her other tormentors, calling on those around her to be silent and dance with her. "Schweigen und tanzen," she sings, dancing herself to death, carrying, as she puts it, "die Last des Glükkes" (the burden of joy). The burden of joy, indeed. In these operas that culminate the trend I have been describing, it is impossible to separate pain from pleasure, sorrow from joy. But that, of course, is where the music comes in.

The music speaks to us directly, communicating emotions around and through the words, and moving us in ways that go back to the earliest human cultures and the most primitive emotions. The music does all this, to be sure, but it does another thing as well, and this may be its most important function in opera. It constantly reminds us that everything we are seeing and hearing is false, is illusion, is, ultimately, a text. For it is textuality and nothing else that transmutes the pains of opera—and those of life as well—into pleasure. The pains of life are real. The pains we encounter in texts are not. They are bearable pains, and they may help us deal with the unbearable ones as well. The expression of sorrow turns that sorrow into textuality, weaves it into forms that we can share with others. Language and other signs are ways of sharing thoughts and feelings, ways of changing thought into feeling and feeling into thought. That is why textuality is so important, and why the teaching of it is a high calling—if we realize that it extends from the ABCs to the high Cs and teachers prepare themselves to cover that full extent in their classrooms.

Send in the Clowns

The most popular single song in Stephen Sondheim's Broadway play *A Little Night Music* (1973), turned out to be "Send in the Clowns," much to the author's surprise. And the play itself was a great success, which I'm sure he found less surprising. It has had revivals on Broadway and also uptown at the New York City Opera, and has been performed on other stages around the world. But this stage play has a unique background, which makes it especially interesting for studies in comparative textuality. The title comes from that of a Mozart serenade for strings, but the story comes from a movie: Ingmar Bergman's *Smiles of a Summer Night* (1955). And the opera has been made into a musical movie version starring Elizabeth Taylor (1977), which actually takes the story back closer to the original film in some respects, but differs from both film and stage versions in others. The medium does affect the message. There is also an imitation of the Bergman film by Woody Allen, called *A Midsummer Night's Sex Comedy* (1982). Bergman himself claimed that his film was derived from a farce by Marivaux from three centuries ago. But Shakespeare's *Midsummer Night's Dream* also lurks in the background of all these modern works. So, which version is the real story?

This question has no answer, I should think, because the story of *A Little Night Music* is a set of words and music that comes alive in performance only—and every performance is different. There is a published version of the verbal script, with a fascinating introduction by Jonathan Tunick, who had the job of turning Hugh Wheeler's book and Stephen Sondheim's piano score and lyrics into something a stage orchestra could play for singing actors and actresses to perform. The collaborative nature of this kind of text is beautifully explained in Tunick's short introduction to the printed text, which also provides information about Sondheim's surprise at the success of "Send in the Clowns" and the fact that this song is written in short lines because the actress who was to sing it couldn't handle long ones. This kind of adaptation isn't new. Mozart, also, would adjust his vocal music to strengths and weaknesses of his performers. But it is interesting to know, nonetheless. Sondheim also revised the lyrics of that song for Barbara Streisand to perform.

Stephen Sondheim and Jonathan Tunick both worked in a musical world that connects the popular theatre and the opera house. Sondheim himself wrote the lyrics for Leonard Bernstein's musical updating of *Romeo and Juliet*: *West Side Story*. Bernstein was another person who moved easily between the concert hall, the opera house, and the popular stage. It would be a great educational result if teachers could help students follow these people across those lines—not as performers, but as interpreters and critics. To study *A Little Night Music* properly, one must read the printed text, listen to the recorded versions, watch the original Bergman film, and look at the filmed version of the play. Doing this can serve to remind us that every printed text of a play is just a verbal score for performances that are interpretations of that original text. And this is just as true of Shakespeare and Sophocles as it is of Sondheim. In this case we can also see the Sondheim play as a revision of the Bergman film, raising the question of whether or not the revision is an improvement on that original.

Reading the printed text of *A Little Night Music* is useful in various ways, especially since there are group songs, in which it is not always easy to follow the words as they are sung, and there is a lot of witty verse—a bit like Byron's clever rhyming in *Don Juan*. Reading the printed text enables us to slow things down and appreciate this verbal play. For example, in act 1, scene 1, Fredrik is musing, musically, about how to persuade his still virginal wife, Anne, to have sex with him. He considers reading to her and runs through a list of possible authors. After dismissing De Sade, Dickens, and Stendhal, he continues this way:

> De Maupassant's candor
> Would cause her dismay.
> The Brontës are grander
> But not very gay.
> Her taste is much blander,

I'm sorry to say,
But is Hans Christian Ander-
Sen ever risqué?

Literature, it turns out, cannot do the trick, and when Fredrik
murmurs in his frustrated sleep the name of his lover of fourteen
years ago, Desirée, and Anne hears it, his troubles begin.

The plot is too complicated to be recounted here, but Jonathan
Tunick's summary will be useful: "A chain of triangles: in each of
these connected relationships, the unstable number three is drawn
to the stable two, as the various mismatched couples disengage and
find their proper partners." One of those proper couples consists of
Fredrik and his former lover, Desirée, but when they have a chance
to talk, late in the play, it looks as if a happy ending is impossible for
them, because Fredrik is still married to his virginal bride, though
Desirée has freed herself of her arrogant lover, Carl-Magnus. Their
sense of this impossibility leads to the song, "Send in the Clowns,"
which begins with these words sung by Desirée:

Isn't it rich?
Are we a pair?
Me here at last on the ground,
You in mid-air.
Send in the clowns.

Desirée is a professional actress, who has played roles from Racine
and Ibsen, and acted in comedies and farces as well, and she rec-
ognizes the farcical side of the situation in which she and Fredrik
have found themselves. As she muses on that situation in theatrical terms, she sees Fredrik and herself as if they were acrobats
in a circus who have missed their connection, and asks for the
clowns to be sent in to cover their mistake. As she thinks it over in
song, however, she comes to this conclusion: "Quick, send in the

clowns. / Don't bother, they're here." That is, she realizes that she and Fredrik are the clowns, imprisoned in their farcical roles. She, as Rebecca West would say, is just an actress who actually never existed, singing to a lawyer, who also never existed, yet we feel for them and are moved by their situation, so that we are ready to accept the happy ending when this farce turns into a comedy at the end. But where did those clowns come from, and how did they get in the play? Actually, they were there in the Bergman film, but in other roles.

There are other happy endings in the play, though they are different from those in the film. The summer night has three smiles in both versions, but they are not all the same. In the opera, Desirée's old mother tells her granddaughter, Fredrika, that there is one smile for the young, one for fools, and one for the old. The smile on the young results in the virginal Anne running off with Fredrik's son Henrik, freeing Fredrik to reunite with Desirée. The smile on the fools results in Desirée and her former lover (who may be Fredrika's father) finally getting together. And the smile on the old results in Fredrika's grandmother dying peacefully on stage at the end of the play. This moment is not in either film version, and the third smile itself is different in the original film as well.

In Bergman's film, the two working-class lovers, Petra and Frid, who have much larger roles than in Sondheim's play, are the fools on whom the midnight sun smiles. It is the groom, Frid, who describes the three smiles of the summer night, and it is Petra and Frid who call themselves clowns. That third smile in the Bergman film is not for the old, but, as Frid puts it, "for the sad, the depressed, the sleepless, the confused, the frightened, the lonely"—which seems to point well beyond the characters in the film. After this speech, the film ends with the maid Petra telling Frid that "the clowns will have a cup of coffee in the kitchen." The play, on the other hand, ends with two happy conclusions. In the first, Fredrik and Desirée embrace, singing "Make way for the clowns. / Applause for the clowns. / They're finally here." And the ultimate ending comes with Madame Armfeldt telling her granddaughter that the smile for the fools was particularly broad that night. Fredrika then says "So there's only the last to come." Her grandmother's reply, "Only the last," gives the play its final happy ending, as she closes her eyes permanently, with the other characters waltzing around the stage behind her. A peaceful death after a full life can indeed be a happy ending—in Sondheim's world and in ours.

For purposes of comparative textuality, the Bergman film and the Sondheim printed text plus the music should be the major objects of interest. Ideally, one should read the text and listen to one of the excellent recorded versions. The film of the play can also be used, but cautiously, as a version of both the earlier texts. Comparing all these can open the way to serious considerations. These works have a lot to say about human emotions and relationships, about what is real and what is unreal in life, about what can be changed and what cannot, about the relationships among love, lust, and marriage. In all of the versions there is a mixture of cynicism and wisdom that invites us to consider what we believe and disbelieve about what we are being told about friendship and love, about sex and marriage, about life and death. We can get to these larger matters by way of specific questions about the texts of the versions.

In the film a Russian roulette duel between Fredrik and Carl-Magnus results in Fredrik getting sprayed with soot, because Carl-Magnus loaded the gun with it, not wanting to risk death in a duel with a mere lawyer. But in the musical the bullet is real, though Fredrik only grazes his own ear with it, instead of putting it into his brain. Asking what difference this makes can take us to interesting places. We might also ask, What is lost or gained by turning Desirée's son Fredrik into her daughter Fredrika in the opera? What is lost or gained by giving some of the cynical wisdom of the groom, Frid, to the grandmother, and some to Petra? How do we feel about Petra's jolly cynicism? And what do we lose when we lose the grandmother's death in the film of the opera? What is lost or gained by allowing Fredrik and Desirée to usurp the position of "clowns" in the shift from film to opera? Is all life a path to disillusionment? And, if so, how do we bear that, except by creating more illusions? Does the music help us face what these texts are saying? Does it enhance the meaning, or does it distract us? What truths, if any, do these beautiful lies contain? Adding Shakespeare's play and Woody Allen's film on this theme to the discussion can only complicate these questions and their answers in interesting ways. Send in the texts!

Put on the Clown Suit

"Vesti la giubba" is the original of the phrase translated above. They are the words of an actor getting ready to go out on stage, but they are not the first words uttered by the clown in question in this dramatic scene from the opera *Pagliacci*. He is talking to himself, and he begins by telling himself to "Perform!" (*Recitar!*). It is time for him to go on stage and make people laugh, although he is delirious (*delirio*) with jealousy and husbandly rage at the infidelity of his performing companion. This moment is built on the difference between real life and performing for an audience. But the singer of these words is performing already, and this whole opera is about the interconnections between performance and reality. The song this actor performs, for himself and the audience of the opera, is one of the most famous in the whole tenor repertory, sung often at recitals and concerts. It was one of Caruso's favorites, and may even have been sung by him when a real clown followed him at one concert and said, "You ain't heard nothin' yet." That clown, Al Jolson, also said those same words more than once in *The Jazz Singer*, starting the "talkies" right there, and changing film forever. There is even a *Pagliacci*-like scene in *The Jazz Singer*, when the singer is in his dressing room, putting on his clownish, blackface makeup, while his mother pleads with him to give up the theatre and come sing in the synagogue for his dying father. The singer counters the appeal to the sacred texts of Judaism with a sacred saying from the theatre world: "The show must go on."

Both *Pagliacci* and *The Jazz Singer* are about the relationship between stage performance and performance in real life. Jonathan Rose has given us useful information not only about naïve reactions to printed narratives but also about such reactions to the theatrical performances.

Of course, as common readers read more widely, they generally learned to read more critically. If John Clare's neighbors believed everything in print, eventually John Clare knew better. Yet when he was confronted with a new medium of expression, Clare could revert to an amazing credulity. Attending a performance of *The Merchant of Venice*, he was so gripped by Portia's judgment that he leapt from the box and assaulted Shylock. That was a common reaction among working class audiences as late as 1900, when farmworker William Miles did a stint with a travelling theater company.

My own father told me about seeing episodes of audience involvement and interruption in theatres well into the twentieth century in America, when he performed in amateur theatricals. The barrier between performance and reality is neither as strong nor as clear as we might wish it to be. And this makes it something to be studied and taught. *Pagliacci*, an opera about a crazy clown is, in fact, a great text for teaching about these matters, since it raises these questions from beginning to end, though the music makes it difficult for us to put on the motley ourselves and leap upon the stage. But the boundary between fiction and reality is part of what the opera *Pagliacci* is all about. The root of the word *pagliaccio* is *paglia*, which means straw. The Scarecrow in Oz is literally a *pagliaccio*, a straw man. The word came to mean a performer in popular comedies, an actor, a person playing a comic role. We may notice that the title of the opera lacks a definite article. One feels that it ought to be *"I Pagliacci," The Clowns*, and it is sometimes mistakenly written that way, but the lack of a definite article is clearly intentional, a part of the meaning of the title. The opera is about all clowns, all performers, not just those engaged in the comic play within the tragic play that is this opera. But we need to look more closely at this aspect of the text.

The verbal part of the opera begins with a man stepping out from behind the curtain and addressing the audience directly. In most performances this man appears wearing the costume of one of the members of a group of traveling players, but he does not address us as that character. Instead, he removes his wig and addresses us as someone else. But who else? If he were the opera singer, come to make an announcement, he would speak rather than sing, but he sings to us instead of speaking, turning this into a performance rather than an announcement. He tells us, however, that he is outside the story, merely a prologue (*"Io sono il Prologo"*). And he straightens from his bent posture and takes off the wig of his character (Tonio) to show us that it is not the character speaking, but someone who is in a zone between the fictional character and the real actor, someone who will assume the role of an even more fictional character, when he performs as the clown called Taddeo in a traditional comedy within the tragic opera. All the levels are important, for this is a meta-opera, a performance that is about performance, and this performer has been given powerful music and important words. He sings to tell us that, contrary to any expectations we may have, what we are about to see is not imaginary, but real—

...L'autore ha cercato invece	(The author has sought instead)
pingervi uno squarcio di vita.	(to sketch a slice of life.)
Egli ha per massimo sol	(He has one rule only)
che l'artista é un uom—	(that the artist is a man—)
e che per gli uomini scrivere ei deve,	(and that he must write for men,)
Ed al vero ispiravasi.	(Inspired by the truth.)
Un nido di memorie in fondo a l'anima	(A nest of memories deep in the soul)
cantavo un giorno	(sang out one day)
ed ei con vere lacrimae scrisse,	(and he wrote with real tears)
e i singhiozzi	(and his sobs)
il tempo gli battavano!	(beat time for him!)

This singing actor is using words written by the composer (who wrote his own libretto) to tell us what lies behind the composition. As it happens, when accused of plagiarism, Leoncavallo responded that his father had been a judge who tried a case that resembled the events of his opera. In any case, this author wants us to believe that his fiction is grounded in reality, despite the layers of fictionality he has imposed upon the events. The prologue tells us that "a nest of memories deep in the soul sang out one day" to the composer, who simply recorded that song. Yet this is one of the most tightly constructed operas in the entire repertory, suggesting anything but an emotional outburst. Who can we trust here? When the speaker of the prologue is finished, he resumes his role, putting his wig back on and returning behind the curtain, which soon opens for the first of the opera's two acts. This move through the real curtain of the opera—from the reality of the audience to the unreality of the stage—is an anticipation of the tenor's move from his reality of pain to the unreality of comedy later on. And one of the points of the opera is that no stage curtain is a hermetic seal.

After the prologue, as the events are enacted before us, we learn that we are watching a group of traveling actors, who perform traditional *commedia dell'arte* in small towns, and that there are tensions among the actors. The only female in the group, Nedda, is apparently married to the leading male, but she is also being hit on by the hunchback who stepped out of character to function as the prologue. She rebuffs the hunchback (Tonio), but is betraying her husband (Canio) with another man (Silvio) who is not a part of the theatrical company. Canio is, at some level, aware of this and troubled by it, but contains his emotions until the rejected Tonio arranges for him to see the lovers together, providing him with ocular proof of Nedda's infidelity.

We have a "real" scene arranged as unwitting performance by an actor playing stage manager of reality, and this scene drives another actor over the edge into what he himself calls "delirio." It is at this point in the opera, when it is time to get ready for the evening performance of the *commedia*, that Canio sings the famous *Vesti la giubba* aria, while preparing to go on stage. "Perform," he tells himself, "laugh, clown, over your broken love, laugh at the pain poisoning your heart." The scene ends with him jerking aside the curtain behind the little stage on which he will enact his clownish role to go out and face the audience. Among the ironies that flow around this text is the role he plays in the *commedia*. He is Pagliaccio, *the* clown of the play, the butt of the jokes, and his role is to be mocked for the sexual betrayal of Columbina, played by his real wife, Nedda. In other words, he is supposed to play for laughs the role of betrayed lover that has been forced on him in his real life as an actor. The burden that makes him delirious is that he is supposed to play exactly what is driving him crazy—but as a comedy. Art and life have come too close together here—so close that they cannot be separated. The part of Columbina calls upon her to speak to her stage lover, Arlecchino, using the same words Canio overheard her saying to her real lover. Perhaps she used them in reality because they expressed her feelings better than any words she could invent. But this is another case of art and life interpenetrating dangerously. When Canio hears these words, he mutters *"Quelle stesse parole!"* (Those same words!) and proceeds to try to force Columbina/Nedda to reveal the name of her real lover.

Silvio is in the audience, watching this, saying "What a strange comedy!" (*Oh, la strana commedia!*) and finally rushing on to the stage to intervene. Delayed by his fellow audience members, he arrives too late. Nedda, trying to run off the stage has been stabbed by Canio, who then stabs Silvio when he reaches the stage, after which Canio drops his knife and stands there. The last words of the opera are *"La commedia e finita"* (The play is over). The libretto calls for them to be spoken by Canio/Pagliaccio, but they are sometimes given to Tonio/Taddeo, the actor who performed the prologue. Whoever speaks them, they function on more than one level. The play within the play is over, and the opera is over. The lives of the characters, which were all tangled up with their roles, are also over or utterly changed. In the inner play Taddeo, played by Tonio, performs the same role he has played in the real lives of the actors, bringing the husband to see the wife's betrayal of him, because she scorns him in the commedia as she has scorned him in the larger drama.

It is worth noting that this opera continues to play its own role in popular culture. For example, there was a Seinfeld episode in the fourth season that involved the main characters' plans to attend a performance of *Pagliacci*. This plan is complicated by various Seinfeldian problems, including determining the proper costume for attendance at the opera, Kramer's lifelong fear of clowns, and Elaine's current boyfriend's madness. Off his meds, apparently, Joe Davola sees himself as Canio, calls Elaine "Nedda" and keeps asking her for the name of his rival until she escapes his clutches. He then dresses up in a clown suit, while playing *Vesti la giubba* on his record player, and makes his own plans to attend the performance. Seinfeldian life is imitating operative art, with a vengeance. Seinfeld is all about roles and the inability of the characters to get out of those they have grown into, no matter how hard they try. It is not so much a show about "nothing" as a show about getting trapped in character. They are all clowns, stuck in roles as fixed as those of commedia dell'arte. George will always be George, Elaine, Elaine, and Kramer, Kramer. Seinfeld himself, in the final credits for this episode is shown in frozen images accompanied on the sound track by *Vesti la giubba*. He, too, is a clown who must perform for his life. And so is the "real" Seinfeld.

Life, it seems offers roles, and people fall into them. That is one reason why the arts can represent life—because life isn't totally real in the first place, though it is in the final analysis. Tonio says that he found Nedda as an orphan, rescued her and offered her his name, which tells us that he saw his life as a scenario in which he had earned a happy ending. But one of the great ancient play-wrights told us to count no one happy until they are dead, meaning that you can't evaluate a life story until it is over. Death is the only closure offered by life, which makes art and life absolutely different, no matter how closely they may resemble one another. This difference is brought home to us by an episode recounted by Jonathan Rose, in which, after a particularly effective death scene, the audience shouts "Die again!", and the actor complies. Encores in opera, outlawed in some opera houses but occasionally allowed anyway, are a remnant of this desire, which is partly a desire for reassurance about the difference between art and life. The show always goes on, but life does not. One great function of artistic texts is to remind us of this, to teach us about life, by resembling it but always remaining that fatal step away.

In these pages I have been trying to explore ways of studying and teaching how our texts and our lives may be connected, believing that understanding this process enhances and enriches those lives. And now this textual comedy is also nearly finished—and the author must remove his own clown suit and retreat to the other side of the textual curtain he has woven, looking, like Madame Armfeldt, for the last smile of a summer night. But the fat lady has yet to sing, allowing this performer one more chance to pull things together before that final smile.

It Ain't Over 'Till the Fat Lady Sings

This expression comes from the world of sports, where it means, roughly, that you should keep trying to win, no matter what the score may be, but it clearly embodies a certain view of opera as a world where funny people do funny things. I first saw the fat lady sing when I was ten or eleven years old, when my grammar school class was taken to the Metropolitan Opera to see Wagner. We were supposed to go to *Siegfried*; we spent preparation time learning about leitmotifs, those musical themes that haunt *The Ring*; and we were looking forward to seeing the dragon, Fafnir, on stage. But there was some kind of mix-up and what we actually saw was *Tristan und Isolde*. All I remember from this production was two large people in bearskins, trying to embrace one another. After that, I stuck to liking it hot, and didn't return to opera until my own love potion led me there ten years later. We sometimes think of opera as an elite form, but, as we have seen, it is connected in various ways to popular theatre, television, and film. Think of the Marx brothers and *A Night at the Opera*, for example.

In this chapter I have been trying to suggest that we can make better use of musical theatre and film, including opera, in teaching textuality. Most people like music; many people know something about it; and quite a few can even read it and play it on some instrument. This situation offers possibilities for the teaching of textuality that can be developed and used to enrich our classrooms. Because many music dramas and films also exist in other forms—as stories, novels, or plays without music, for example, or as videos and librettos—they offer splendid opportunities for comparative textuality. If, for example, we follow Bernard Shaw's play *Pygmalion* from its written text, to the film version with a "Hollywood" ending approved by Shaw, to its musical incarnation as *My Fair Lady*, we can move easily to questions of interpretation and criticism, including criticism of performances as interpretations of the original text. We can compare Wendy Hiller's rendition of Eliza Doolittle in the spoken film to that of Audrey Hepburn in the musical version and ask which performance of that role captures the character better, which can lead to the question of what that character is all about in the first place. And we can compare the endings of the original play and the two later versions, asking whether marriage to an academic is really a happy ending for Eliza. We can also push comparative textuality further, comparing Eliza as a character with Lola-Lola and Sugar.

It would also be an excellent idea to read Christopher Isherwood's two books about his experiences in Berlin in the 1930s (*The Last of Mr. Norris* and *Goodbye to Berlin*); to read the stage version of those books, *I Am a Camera*, by John Van Druten; to look at the film of that version; and to compare these with the musical *Cabaret*, which ultimately became a film as well, finally linking all these texts to *The Blue Angel*. Sally Bowles, though based on a real person, is also a descendant of the fictional Lola-Lola in the earlier film. Studying multimedia texts like these opens the way to cultural and social history by way of textuality. In the case of Isherwood's Berlin, we can also turn to his later memoir of those years, *Christopher and His Kind*, which reveals things concealed in the first two novels about that period of his life. Comparison of all these texts can teach all concerned something about the interpretation and criticism of narrative works. Is the memoir the real story, the last word? Is it the most interesting version of Isherwood's life in those years? How does it change the way we read the other versions? Students can be asked which version they like best, which they believe most, which they have learned the most from—and why. Which one tells us the most about that place and time? Which one tells us the most about Christopher Isherwood?

Which one would we miss most if we did not have it? And which one is most satisfying as a story? What does the music do for this story, along with the other elements that turn it into something properly called *Cabaret*? What is gained, and what is lost, by this focus on performance?

Comparative textuality of this sort embodies a more spacious idea of literacy than a concern with literary works alone. If we visualize textual studies as built around a center of those texts given sacred status in our culture—whether religious or political—and extending outward in various directions, this can lead us to two conclusions: first, that the sacred texts must be studied, interpreted, and criticized; and, second, that coverage will not work for the entire world of textuality, which is just too big, and too various, to be covered realistically. Moving beyond the sacred texts, what students need are textual experiences that will increase their own textual power and extend the range of their textual pleasures. To accomplish this we need a concept of textuality that can include everything from a magazine ad promoting a cure for lice in children's hair to a poem like Schiller's "Ode to Joy," which is the verbal text for the conclusion of Beethoven's *Ninth Symphony*. And that is why, in this chapter, I have been arguing for the use of music drama as a resource in the teaching of comparative textuality. It is far from being the only such resource, but its possibilities are great, and they are largely neglected in our fallen academic world. Our "wandring steps and slow," in my opinion, need to be warmed up with a little night music.

Having drawn my conclusions, I believe I can hear the fat lady beginning to sing. But who is she? And what is she singing? I think she must be a Wagnerian soprano, and that thought takes me back seventy years, to that little boy who was hoping for a dragon and got the fat lady instead—and learned to love her in another life. For me, the fat lady must be Isolde, standing over the body of her dead lover, Tristan, seeing him as if he were alive, while she dies herself, singing to the most orgasmic orchestral music ever written. She believes she is hearing a melody emerging from within Tristan's body, a melody in which she is blissfully drowning. The last word sung by the fat lady is "joy."

A Sample Program in Textuality

In this book I have been trying to teach about teaching, or—as Wittgenstein might have put it—to teach the unteachable. I have tried, perversely, to show that we need to use our creative powers to interpret sacred texts as closely as possible, imagining the intentions of their creators, and to use our critical powers to tease out the values hidden in profane texts, so as to see what we may learn from them about our own lives. In all of this, I have assumed that reading is a constructive process, a kind of writing, whether it ends up in images in the mind, in sounds in the air, in pixels on a screen, or ink on a page. Learning to re-weave the texts we encounter in the texts of our lives is the process I have been trying to describe, and, in particular, I have tried to show how teachers may share this process with students. All this has a practical side, as well, and in this epilogue I will offer some advice in that direction. But first, a personal anecdote.

As I was finishing this book, I was visited by three people I had taught as undergraduates fifty years ago at the University of Virginia. In one case, I had advised a young man to change his major from math to English. He had asked what he could do with an English major. I had replied that he could go to law school. He did just that and had a successful career as a lawyer. Another had told me he wanted to go to divinity school and become a minister. I did everything I could to talk him out of that, lending him books about ministers by James Gould Cozzens, Sinclair Lewis, and others. He ignored my advice, and had a very satisfying career as a minister. In the case of the third student, I don't recall ever giving him career advice, but he went to graduate school, got a PhD in English, and had an excellent career as a professor. But they were all grateful to me—not for what I had advised them to do but because I had cared about them and cared about what I was teaching. Which means, as I understand it, that the recommendations that follow here will be useful only to people who care about their students and care about the texts they share with those students. If they don't care about the curriculum I propose, they should invent another one that they do care about. The essential matter for teachers of textuality is to get the interpretation of sacred texts into the curriculum, and to help students take pleasurable texts seriously—and to care about both the texts and the students. Here, then, is a program that I could care about.

This is not an ideal program but an attempt to describe something that is actually possible within the framework of existing departments. Even so, it is probably more than many schools are likely to attempt. I hope, however, that it may be sufficiently realistic for English departments to consider—if they are creative enough or desperate enough, or both. What follows here is a suggestion for a core of courses to be followed by advanced work drawn from whatever curriculum is already in place in a given institution. It is just a suggestion, however. There are many ways to do this. But we need to find better ways to help students think about critical interpretation and what is at stake in reading important texts. The idea is that students who have gone through this core will learn more from standard courses than students who have not had this core experience. The core will ensure a grounding in textuality: reading and writing with some sophistication. The language requirement will enhance these skills. And the introduction to modernism will provide a framework for viewing earlier (and later) forms of cultural production. The basic courses should be open to all students, replacing (or competing with) the standard composition and introduction to literature options.

To actually generate a program like this, given the current divisions in programs and departments, it might be necessary to make it interdepartmental, involving English, Media, and Comparative Literature, for example—but it can be done, if the energy and willpower are there to do it.

$\sim$

LANGUAGE REQUIREMENT (not a prerequisite)
Reading proficiency in an ancient language or a modern language other than English

BASIC COURSES

1. A writing course, of course. But every member of the department should teach one, and the sections should be small enough for the individual attention that writing instruction requires. This course should be writing about reading. That is, all instructors should design a set of readings in which they are interested themselves—interested enough to get students to share that interest. It can be writing about film, or writing about poetry, or writing the personal essay, or writing about advertising. An instructor at Brown (Jonathan Goldman) had good success with a "Writing About *Ulysses*" section of a basic writing course. But every section should be clearly described so that students can choose what they want to write about as well as who they want to study with, and when they want to be in class. In the Department of Modern Culture and Media at Brown a few years ago, a teaching assistant and I offered two sections of a course called "Textuality," in which we used a book put together by Nancy Comley, Greg Ulmer, and myself, called *Text Book*. This book breaks the line between creative and noncreative forms of writing and offers a range of challenging and playful assignments.

This book, or one of its imitators, might work well. But choice is very important in the success of such a course. Instructors must choose their topics, and students select topics that interest them. In the sections, students should write a lot, and get feedback from one another as well as from the instructor. Digital methods of communication can work well in writing courses.

2. Reading Sacred Texts (theories of interpretation and canonicity with readings in religious and political texts). This course should explore notions of "literal" and "strict" reading, intentionality, and the designation of texts as "sacred" or "special." Some discussion of literary "canonicity" and literary interpretation may be included but should not dominate. The main function of this course should be to emphasize the distance between the originators of such texts and ourselves, as a way of helping students avoid the tendency to impose their own views on whatever they read. The place for one's own views comes after understanding the views embodied in the text, and this is an important lesson that we all need to learn over and over again. The course ought to be writing-intensive, with small sections, though it could work with a large lecture combined with small workshops that emphasize discussion and writing. Guest lectures by faculty from religious and political departments might work very well for this purpose.

INTERMEDIATE COURSES

3. An Ancient Culture Course. For example, Histor and Rhetor: Aristotle's *Rhetoric*, and readings in ancient historians (Herodotus, Xenophon, Thucydides, Livy, Tacitus—looking at the rhetoric of speeches, for example, in the historical texts, and the tension between rhetoric and history that exists in them). The purpose of a course like this is to get students thinking about the ancient world, and the way that the concept of history developed in connection with and opposition to notions of rhetoric. (I

taught a version of "Histor and Rhetor" at Iowa in the late 60s. It went quite well.) An alternative might be Aristotle's *Poetics* and "Longinus on the Sublime," with readings in ancient drama. But the main point is to allow students to enter a world very different from our own and consider a coherent body of works from that world, including works that take a critical or theoretical stance about the form of textual production being considered—as Aristotle's *Rhetoric* and *Poetics* do.

4. Comparative Textuality (a range of texts selected in order to illustrate how interpretive methods apply across the media—and how they must be modified). In particular, texts that have crossed media, like Shakespeare's *Othello* and Verdi's *Otello*, or Isherwood's Berlin stories and *Cabaret*, belong in such a course. Situating texts in their historical and cultural context must be a part of this process, which means that texts from different times and places should be considered. This asks participating faculty to have some range, which runs counter to current modes of specialization, but I think it is healthy. Many of our faculty are less narrow in their interests than they may seem to be.

5. Understanding Modernism (debates, manifestos, examples, using magazine resources, such as the *New Age*, *Rhythm*, *Blast*, the *Egoist*, the *Little Review*, *Poetry*, the *Crisis*). In this course modernism may be presented as a set of literary works that are published along with their supporting manifestos and arguments about them. Topics such as imagism (or *imagisme*), futurism, vorticism, and the debates that surrounded them should be covered. But modernism also includes social and political movements, like the push for women's suffrage or racial justice. In movements like futurism, the political was never far from the artistic. Modernism was the filter through which the cultures of the past came to our own time, shaping the way we perceive them, which gives it a special place in a textual curriculum. This course will have to be taught by people with training in the field, but their interests

should not be confined to America or Britain. Modernism was an international phenomenon.

ADVANCED COURSES

These can be drawn from currently available courses, with whatever requirements for distribution across historical periods, genres, languages, and media seem appropriate, drawn from a range of relevant departments. Connections to modern and contemporary culture should be made in all these courses. For example, a study of eighteenth-century British literature should not ignore advertising in the *Spectator*, which anticipates modern advertising in many ways. And a course in Shakespeare should consider the ways his plays have been adapted for such other media as opera and film.

A NOTE ON SOURCES

The printed works I consulted in writing this book are listed below, but I want to mention specifically here some texts used with special frequency or intensity. First of all, I want to acknowledge Samuel Johnson, who has been with me since I encountered him in my junior year at Yale and wrote a parody of his style which pleased my teacher more than anything of my own. Johnson's pleasure in agreeing with "the common reader" about Gray's "Elegy Written in a Country Churchyard" taught me a lot. Though I have not always agreed with Johnson, I have always learned from him, and from Boswell's account of his conversation. Also regularly with me in this book is Ezra Pound, with whom I seldom agree, but who always makes me think. He was a master teacher. The epigraph to this book comes from a book about modernism called *The Pound Era*.

Looking in another direction, I have borrowed from my own earlier books in ways that should be acknowledged here: using some material from *The Crafty Reader* in chapter 4, and some from *Modernism in the Magazines* in chapter 3. The roots of many of the ideas developed here lie in those books and in such others as *Textual Power*, *Protocols of Reading*, and *Semiotics and Interpretation*. I am grateful to the Yale University Press for permission to use all this material. I have also drawn frequently on the digital editions of The Modernist Journals Project (www.modjourn.org). My work on these modernist magazines has given me a richer and deeper understanding of modernism than I had previously managed to attain. It was this work that kept bringing Pound to my attention.

Jonathan Rose's extraordinary book, *The Intellectual Life of the British Working Classes*, has also influenced my thinking on textuality. Rose's book is present in this book sometimes, even where it is not visible. The advertising in the serial edition of Dickens's *Bleak House* was drawn to my attention by Emily Steinlight—first in the classroom and then in her article in the list of works consulted, below. And the Hebrew text and translation in chapter 4 were supplied by Lori Lefkovitz, who is expert in these matters. Finally, since this is indeed a sequel to my earlier *Rise and Fall of English*, many of the ideas in this book are extensions or refinements of things discussed in that work. I hope the case has been made more clearly and persuasively this time.

In closing, I should note that I have not listed below all the recordings I listened to and videos I watched in working on this book. One must always get the best of these that are available.

WORKS CONSULTED

Adorno, Theodor. *In Search of Wagner*, Rodney Livingstone, trans. London: Verso, 1985.

Auden, W. H. *The English Auden*, Edward Mendelson, ed. New York: Random House, 1977.

Bauer-Lechner, Natalie. *Erinnerungen an Gustav Mahler*. Leipzig: E. P. Tal & Co, 1923.

———. *Recollections of Gustav Mahler*, Peter Franklin, ed., Dike Newlin, trans. Cambridge: Cambridge University Press, 1980.

Bellah, James Warner. *The Man Who Shot Liberty Valance*. New York: Permabooks, 1962.

Bergman, Ingmar. *Four Screenplays of Ingmar Bergman*, Lars Malstrom and David Kushner, trans. New York: Simon and Schuster, 1960.

Besant, Walter, and Henry James. *The Art of Fiction*. Boston: Cupples, Upham, 1885.

Boswell, James. *The Life of Samuel Johnson, LL. D.* New York: Oxford University Press, 1948.

Brake, Laurel. *Print in Transition, 1850–1910*. New York: Palgrave, 2001.

Burke, Edmund. *A Philosophical Enquiry into the Origin of Our Ideas of the Sublime and the Beautiful*. New York: Oxford University Press, 1990.

Coleridge, Samuel Taylor. *The Best of Coleridge*. New York: Ronald Press, 1934.

Finkelstein, David, ed. *Print Culture and the Blackwood Tradition 1805–1930*. Toronto: University of Toronto Press, 2006.

Frost, Robert. "Design," from *A Further Range*. New York: Henry Holt, 1936.

Graham, William. *The Beginnings of English Literary Periodicals*. New York: Oxford University Press.

Heyward, Dorothy, and Dubose Heyward. *Porgy: A Play in Four Acts*. Garden City: Doubleday, 1928.

———. *Porgy: A Play in Four Acts*, William-Alan Landes, ed. Studio City: Players Press, 2005.

Heyward, DuBose. *Porgy*. Garden City: Doubleday, 1953.

Johnson, Dorothy M. *Indian Country*. New York: Ballantine Books, 1965.

Joyce, James. *Ulysses*. New York: Random House, 1961.

Kames, Henry Home, Lord. *Elements of Criticism*. New York: Johnson Reprint Corporation, 1967.

Kenner, Hugh. *The Pound Era*. Berkeley: University of California Press, 1973.

King, Andres, and John Plunkett, eds. *Victorian Print Media: A Reader*. New York: Oxford University Press, 2006.

Kohlenberger, John. *The Precise Parallel New Testament: Greek Text, King James Version, Rheims Bible, New International Version, New Revised Standard Version, New American Bible, New American Standard Bible, Amplified Bible*. New York: Oxford University Press, 1995.

Korsten, F. J. M. "The 'English Men of Letters' Series: A Monument of Late-Victorian Literary Criticism." *English Studies*: 73.6: 503–516.

Kuhn, Thomas. *The Structure of Scientific Revolutions*. Chicago: University of Chicago Press, 1962.

Latham, Sean. *The Art of Scandal: Modernism, Libel Law, and the Roman à Clef*. New York: Oxford University Press, 2009.

Leavis, F. R. *For Continuity*. Cambridge: Minority Press, 1933.

————. *The Great Tradition*. London: Chatto and Windus, 1948.

Leavis, Q. D. *Fiction and the Reading Public*. London: Chatto and Windus, 1932.

Lewis, Charlton T., and Charles Short. *A Latin Dictionary: Founded on Andrews' Edition of Freund's Latin Dictionary: Revised, Enlarged, and in Great Part Rewritten by Charlton T. Lewis, Ph.D. and Charles Short, LL.D.* New York: Oxford University Press, 1980.

Mahler, Gustav. *Des Knaben Wunderhorn and the Rückert Lieder for Voice and Piano*. Mineola, N.Y.: Dover Publications, 1999.

Mann, Heinrich. *Small Town Tyrant*. New York: Creative Age Press, 1944.

————, and Josef von Sternberg. *The Blue Angel*. New York: Ungar Film Library, 1979.

Marx, Karl. *Critique of Hegel's "Philosophy of Right."* Cambridge: Cambridge University Press, 1977.

Miller, James E. *Theory of Fiction: Henry James*. Lincoln: University of Nebraska Press, 1972.

Milton, John. *Paradise Lost*. University of Virginia, Electronic Text Center.

Pound, Reginald. *Mirror of the Century*. New York: A. S. Barnes, 1966.

Rose, Jonathan. *The Intellectual Life of the British Working Classes*. New Haven: Yale University Press, 2002.

Scholes, Robert. *The Crafty Reader*. New Haven: Yale University Press, 2001.

————. *Protocols of Reading*. New Haven: Yale University Press, 1991.

————. *The Rise and Fall of English*. New Haven: Yale University Press, 1998.

————. *Semiotics and Interpretation*. New Haven: Yale University Press, 1983.

————. *Textual Power*. New Haven: Yale University Press, 1985.

————, and James Phelan. *The Nature of Narrative*. New York: Oxford University Press, 2006.

————, and Clifford Wulfman. *Modernism in the Magazines: An Introduction*. New Haven: Yale University Press, 2010.

Sondheim, Stephen, and Hugh Wheeler. *A Little Night Music*. New York: Applause Theatre and Cinema Books, 1990.

Steinlight, Emily. "'Anti-Bleak House': Advertising and the Victorian Novel." *Narrative*: 14.2 (2006): 132–162.

Van Zuilen, A. J. *The Life Cycle of Popular Magazines*. Uithoorn: Graduate Press, 1977.

Wepman, Dennis. "DuBose Heyward," in *Invisible Giants*, Mark Carnes, ed. New York: Oxford University Press, 2002.

West, Rebecca. *Black Lamb and Grey Falcon*. New York: Penguin Books, 1994.

Wordsworth, William. "London, 1802" from *Poetical Works*. New York: Oxford University Press, 1933.

Yeats, William Butler. *Yeats's Poetry, Drama and Prose*. New York: Norton, 2000.

Corbiau, Gérard: *Le Maître de Musique*, 111

criticism: defined, 51; enabled by comparative textuality, 92; moving beyond interpretation, 71, 81; as third phase of reading, 51–52

crucifixion, 60–61

culture, xvi, 10, 35, 37, 123, 144–145

Declaration of Independence, 36, 79–85; interpreted, 79–85; not literature in English studies, 37; as sacred text needing interpretation, 53–54; as U. S.'s most sacred text, 77

"Design" (Frost), 16–18

Dickens, Charles: *Bleak House*, 45–46

Dietrich, Marlene: singing "Falling in Love Again," 103; in *The Blue Angel*, 100–104

Dobson, Austin, 6–7

Domingo, Placido: in Verdi's *Otello*, 90

Don Giovanni (Mozart), 111–112; *"Or sai chi l'onore,"* 116

Donizetti, Gaetano, 119

Elektra (Strauss), 123–124

Eliot, T. S., xvi–xvii, 8, 11

English: as academic field of study, xiii–xix; curriculum, xiii, 43, 47–48, 50, 89, 142; fall of, xiii–xv, 37; re-orienting, xviii–xix, 31, 34, 37–38, 48–50, 141–146; rise of, xv–xvi

English departments, 15, 33, 142; challenges today, xiv; debt to modernism, xvi, 11; declining enrollments, xiv; hierarchical structure, 33; need

to historicize cultural studies, 47–48; primary mission, xv, 34; rise of, xv–xvi, 10–11; textuality as new focus, xviii–xix

enthymemic form, 20–21

Ernani (Verdi), 118

essay: excluded from literature, 23–24, 33; as literature, 10

explaining (rhetorical category), 15

explication, xvi. *See also* interpretation

"Falling in Love Again" (Hollaender), 103

Falstaff (Verdi), 116

fancy, 5–6

Fanfaren der Liebe (Fanfares of Love): inspiration for *Some Like It Hot*, 106

fiction: as art, 7–8; connection with journalism, 9–10; historical concept of, 107–108; and literature, 6, 10–11; and operatic incarnations, 91; and reality, 94, 105, 108, 131–135

Fielding, Henry, 7

films. See individual film titles

Ford, John: *The Man Who Shot Liberty Valance*, 36–42

Freud, Sigmund, 62

Frost, Robert: "Design," 16–18

fundamentalism, 60–71; and gender inequality, 63–71; what it cannot allow, 71

fundamentalist reading, 54, 62–63, 67–71; of the Bible, 63–67. *See also* strict judicial construction; textualist reading

(Paul on women teaching), 69; 2
Timothy 4:1–7 (Paul on religious
faith), 25–28, 76
Newsom, Carol A.: *The Women's Bible
Commentary*, 69–70
Nietzsche, Friedrich, 122–123
A Night at the Opera, 137

O'Connor, T. P., 8–9
"Ode to Joy" (Schiller), 139
"Oh, Doctor Jesus" (Gershwin),
98–99. *See also Porgy and Bess*
"Oh Lawd, I'm on My Way" (Gershwin), 97. *See also Porgy and Bess*
Old Testament, 55, 67, 96; Deuteronomy 7:2–6 (advice for God's
chosen people), 86; different from
our world, 57; Exodus 20:1–6, 20:17
(Ten Commandments), 54–58;
Genesis 1:27 (problematic word
for God), 67; Genesis 1:27 and
2:21–23 compared (two versions of
creation), 65; multiple authorship
of, 59
opera, 115–124, 130–140; *Arabella*
(Strauss), 116; artificiality, 91; "bel
canto," 119, 121; castrati in, 118; *Don
Giovanni* (Mozart), 111–112, 116;
Elektra (Strauss), 123–124; *Ernani*
(Verdi), 118; *Falstaff* (Verdi), 116;
function of music in, 124; *L'elisir
d'amore* (Donizetti), 116; *Madama
Butterfly* (Puccini), 122; *The Marriage of Figaro* (Mozart), 30, 116,
118–119; as most profane medium,
115; as neglected resource in teaching, 91; operatic pain, 118–119, 122;

Otello (Verdi), 90; *Pagliacci* (Leoncavallo), 130–136; pain and pleasure
interwoven in, 115, 123–124; pedagogical uses for, 90–92; pleasure
of, 117, 123; rejection of sacred
status, 91; *Rigoletto* (Verdi), 107;
Ring Cycle (Wagner), 119–123; *Der
Rosenkavalier* (Strauss), 116; *Salome*
(Strauss), 123; in *Some Like It Hot*,
107; songs in, 123; *Tosca* (Puccini),
122; treated as a text, 92; *Tristan
und Isolde* (Wagner), 122–123,
137, 139–140; women's voices in,
117–118. *See also* music drama
"The Orators" (Auden), 62
Otello (Verdi), 90, 145

"Pacesetter English" (course), 90
Pagliacci (Leoncavallo), 130–136; performance and reality in, 130–136;
prologue of, 132–133; in *Seinfeld*,
135–136; "Vesti la giubba" (aria),
130, 134–136
Paradise Lost (Milton), xiii–xiv, xviii
Paul, Saint, 26–29, 31, 58, 63–76; on
being "all things to all men" (1
Corinthians 9:20–22), 58–59; conversion from force to rhetoric,
72–76; epistles as literature (2
Timothy 4:7), 25–28; feel for Greek
language, 26; on inequality of men
and women (1 Corinthians 11:3–11),
65–67; as master rhetorician, 21, 70,
75; on reading according to "the
spirit" (2 Corinthians 3:6), 68; on
religious faith (2 Timothy 4:1–7),
25–28, 76; on rules for women's

clothing, 67–69; as Saul of Tarsus
(Acts 7–16), 72–76; shift in narrative
voice (Acts 16:8–10), 74; textualist
reading of, 70–71; on wives' sub-
jection to husbands (Ephesians
5:22–23), 64; on women speaking
in church (1 Corinthians 14:34–35),
69; on women teaching (1 Timothy 2:11–12), 69

Pavarotti, Luciano, 118

performance, 26, 34, 91–93, 102; and
gender, 105; as interpretation, 92,
126, 138; nature of, 93; power of,
103–104; *Some Like It Hot* as comedy
about, 105; on stage and in real life,
93, 130–132

persuasive discourse, 19–21. *See also*
rhetoric

Petrarch (Francesco Petrarca), 16

poetry: not considered serious in
seventeenth century, 2; political
effect, 24; as rhetoric, 16; sonnets, 16–23; usefulness in writing
courses, 15–23

Porgy and Bess, 91, 94–100; as disturbing work of naturalism, 96;
as novel, stage play, and music
drama, 96; source of Porgy's character, 108

Pound, Ezra, 11, 147–148; *How to Read*,
10; on Milton, 21; "Studies in Contemporary Mentality," 43–44

print culture, 36, 38

print media, 11, 33, 38, 45, 47, 49

profane texts, 89–140; and allevia-
tion of pain, 90; and comparative
textuality, 91; defined, 89; music

drama and opera, 90–91; tension
with the sacred in, 93–100; and textual pleasure, 89–140

Puccini, Giacomo: *Madama Butterfly*,
122; *Tosca*, 122

Quran (2:190–193), 87

Raphaelson, Samson: "The Day of
Atonement," 94. See also *The Jazz
Singer*

reaction, 50–51

reading: as imaginative recreation of
text, 35; of profane texts, 89–140;
of sacred texts, 53–88; teaching of,
15, 33–52; three phases of, 50–52;
by working class, 107–108. *See also*
fundamentalist reading; textualist
reading

realistic novel, 108

reflecting, 15; in Frost's "Design,"
16–17

reporting, 15; in Frost's "Design,"
16–17

rhetoric: Acts of the Apostles as,
74–75; advertisements as, 44; in
Ancient Culture course, 144; and
composition / writing, xv, 17, 21;
and force, 76; four categories of, 15;
in Frost's "Design," 16–17; and history, 144–145; replaced by English
literature, xvi, 11; and Saint Paul,
26–28, 70–72, 75–76; and textuality, 11; in Wordsworth's "London,
1802," 19–21

Richardson, Samuel, 6–7

Rigoletto (Verdi): in *Le Maître de*